ALSO BY MEYER SCHAPIRO

Romanesque Art, Selected Papers, Vol. I

Modern Art, Selected Papers, Vol. II

Late Antique, Early Christian, and Medieval Art, Selected Papers, Vol. III

Theory and Philosophy of Art: Style, Artist, and Society, Selected Papers, Vol. IV

Mondrian: On the Humanity of Abstract Painting

The Bibliography of Meyer Schapiro
edited by Lillian Milgram Schapiro

WORDS, SCRIPT, AND PICTURES:

Semiotics of Visual Language

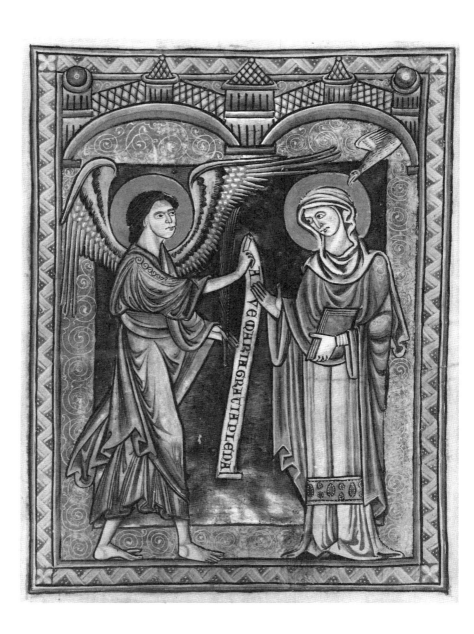

WORDS, SCRIPT, AND PICTURES:

Semiotics of Visual Language

by

MEYER SCHAPIRO

GEORGE BRAZILLER
New York

First published in the United States in 1996 by George Braziller, Inc.
Text copyright © The Estate of Meyer Schapiro, 1996.

For information, please address the publisher:

George Braziller, Inc.
171 Madison Avenue
New York, New York 10016

Library of Congress Cataloging-in-Publication Data:
Schapiro, Meyer, 1904-96
Words, script, and pictures: semiotics of visual language / Meyer Schapiro.
p.   cm.
ISBN 0-8076-1416-5
1. Visual communication.   2. Semiotics   I. Title.
P93.5.S33   1996   96-18996
302.23'014—dc20   CIP

Frontispiece: The Pierpont Morgan Library, New York, G.25, f.1v.
Frontispiece photo: David A. Loggie
Design: Rita Lascaro

Printed and bound in the United States

First edition

CONTENTS

ACKNOWLEDGMENTS

The substance of "Words and Pictures: On the Literal and the Symbolic in the Illustration of a Text" was presented at a symposium, "Language, Symbol, Reality," held at St. Mary's College, Notre Dame, Indiana, on November 7, 1969, and an earlier version in a lecture to the Seminar on Hermeneutics at Columbia University in April 1960. For help in the preparation of the text, I wish to thank Dr. Miriam Bunim. —*Meyer Schapiro*

The material in "Script in Pictures: Semiotics of Visual Language" was first presented at a University of Pittsburgh symposium in honor of Carl Nordenfalk on November 18, 1976. It has subsequently been revised.

We would like to thank Dr. Lillian Milgram Schapiro for her gracious assistance during the preparation of this volume.

—*The Publishers*

WORDS
AND
PICTURES:

*On the Literal and the Symbolic
in the Illustration of a Text*

Chapter 1

THE ARTIST'S
READING OF A TEXT

A great part of visual art in Europe from late antiquity to the 18th century represents subjects taken from a written text. The painter and sculptor had the task of translating the word—religious, historical, or poetic—into a visual image. It is true that many artists did not consult the text but copied an existing illustration either closely or with some change. But for us today the intelligibility of that copy, as of the original, rests finally on its correspondence to a known text through the recognizable forms of the pictured objects and actions signified by the words. The picture, we assume further, corresponds to the concept or memory image associated with the words.

That correspondence of word and picture is often problematic and may be surprisingly vague. In old printed Bibles the same woodcut was used sometimes to illustrate different subjects. These, however, were episodes with a common general meaning.

The picture of Jacob's birth was repeated for the birth of Joseph and other scriptural figures, and a battle scene was serviceable for illustrating several such encounters. It is the place of the woodcut in the book, at a certain point in the text, that permits us to grasp the more specific meaning.

Yet in other cases, seeing in a picture only a few elements from a known text, we are able to identify the story. The text is often so much fuller than the illustration that the latter seems a mere token, like a pictorial title: one or two figures and some attribute or accessory object, seen together, will evoke for the instructed viewer the whole chain of actions linked in that text with the few pictured elements, unless an incompatible detail arrests the inter-pretation. Examples are the paintings in the Christian catacombs of Rome where Noah stands in the ark, Daniel between lions, and Susanna beside the elders. But the meaning of such reductive imagery may be rich in connotations and symbolized values not evident from the basic text itself; these were fixed for the Christian viewer by what he had learned about the same themes from religious commentary and allusions in sermons, ritual, and prayer. Today that fuller meaning has to be recovered through a search of the old writings and contexts; and when we have come to know these, it still remains uncertain which of the various meanings of the subject, embedded in the literary elaborations of the basic text, was intended in a particular labeled image.

Take as an example the episodes from the Old Testament that I have just mentioned. They appear together in prayers in both the synagogue and church as instances of God's intervention to save the faithful in mortal danger. Scholars have explained the choice of those subjects for paintings in the catacombs and for sculptures on sarcophagi as appropriate to the idea of deliverance. But a Greek Christian theologian of the same period, Hippolytus of Rome, interpreted the story of Susanna in another and more complex way in the exegetical style of the time. Susanna, he wrote, is the persecuted church; her husband, Joachim, is Christ; their garden is the society of the saints who are like fruitful trees; Babylon, which surrounds the garden, is the world in which Christians live; the two elders are the two peoples, the Jews and the pagans, who are enemies of the church; Susanna's bath is the water of Baptism that regenerates the church on Easter day; the two maidservants are faith and charity; the perfumes they apply to their mistress's body are the commandments of the Word; and the oil is the grace of the Holy Spirit, especially that which is conferred by confirmation.[1]

Turn now to the catacomb paintings of Susanna and the Elders. We usually see only these three figures on a bare ground; none of the other elements of the story as told in the Book of Daniel is represented.[2] In one example Susanna is replaced by a sheep and the elders become two wolves with the inscription *seniores*. The wolves are metaphors that might have a theological sense, for "wolf" is also a term for heretic. But the wolves are intelligible here through the Gospel as figures for evil (Matthew 10:16), and knowing other examples of scenes from the Scriptures represented through animal actors, we are satisfied to accept the usual reading of the metaphorical picture as a symbol of deliverance. But we cannot exclude the possibility of other meanings for Christians of that time.

If some illustrations of a text are extreme reductions of a complex narrative—a mere emblem of the story—others enlarge the text, adding details, figures, and a setting not given in the written source. Sometimes the text itself is not specific enough to determine a picture, even in the barest form. Where the Book of Genesis tells that Cain killed Abel, one can hardly illustrate the story without showing how the murder was done. But no weapon is mentioned in the text and the artists have to invent the means. Both the Hebrew *vayahargahu,* "killed him," and its Latin equivalent *interfecit eum* are general terms referring to the effect rather than to the action as such. Yet even the effect here cannot be pictured with both the agent and the victim unless the weapon is shown. Christian folklore and the legends in the Hebrew Midrashim supplied the instrument: a stone, a branch of a tree, a club, a scythe, a jawbone, and still others.[3] Each of these had its ground in the imagined circumstance of the action or even in the name of Cain. It may be a stone because one supposed that the crime was done before there were weapons of iron or bronze; or, remembering that Cain was a farmer, the artist gave him a scythe or hoe. It would seem to follow that the visual image is more concrete than the word; but while this is true in many instances, one can point to verbal accounts with elements of description, physical and psychological, that are not found in the pictures or cannot in principle be translated in all styles of art because of the limited range of their means of representation. In the archaic periods of classic and medieval art painters often felt impelled to inscribe their paintings with the names of the figures and even with phrases identifying the action, although according to a common view, supported by the authority of church fathers, pictures were a mute preaching addressed to the illiterate.

Besides the differences between text and picture arising from the conciseness or generality of the word and from the resources peculiar to verbal and visual art, there are historical factors to consider: (a) the changes in meaning of a text for successive illustrators, though the words remain the same, and (b) the changes in style of representation, which affect the choice of details and their expressive import.

The change of meaning may have different causes. In the pictorial version the original text was often conflated with or contaminated by other texts and images. So in the rendering of the Nativity the familiar and in practice canonical ox and ass have been introduced from a passage of Isaiah (1:3): "The ox knows his owner and the ass his master's crib; but Israel does not know"—a text that perhaps served the Christian polemic against the Jews who would not acknowledge that Christ was the Messiah and thereby forfeited the sense of their Judaic name as the people who know. So too, a fine theological point may determine a detail in the illustration of a text which in itself provides no literal ground for that feature. In pictures of the pentecostal Descent of the Holy Spirit, the Western artists, in accord with the teaching of the Roman Church and in opposition to Greek Orthodox doctrine, represent the dove descending from the figure of Jesus Christ as well as from the hand of God the Father—a pictorial statement of the *filioque* that separated the two churches.

For the stylistic factor one may point to the great changes in the imaging of traditional Biblical themes that arose from the norms of Byzantine, Romanesque, Gothic, Renaissance, Mannerist, and Baroque art, each with its own mode of representing action and the setting of a scene. The style as a distinctive habitual system of artistic forms is an expressive vehicle and can modify the often scanty literal sense in the very process of translating the text into an image, especially where the text is the creation of a much older and in some ways more primitive type of art. In each style are rules of representation which, together with the ideas and values paramount in the culture, direct the choice of position, posture, gesture, dress, size, milieu, and other features of the actors and objects. In giving a pictorial form to figures named in an old text, the painter often represents them anachronistically as people of his own time and place or according to current ideas about the past. No less than the contemporary interests by which the text is colored in the reading, the style of art pervades and remakes what is taken from the text. And with each new style there is a characteristic trend of the imagination in conceiving a subject. The Adoration of the Magi, known through a Gospel that does not even number the wise men, is represented at first simply by two, three, or four figures in similar Oriental dress advancing to the seated Mary and Child in an undefined space. Later it becomes an elaborate festive scene in a deep landscape with an immense procession of the retinue of three individualized kings and embodies a wealth of allusions acquired through the fantasy of inspired readers and exegetes; written accounts of the story are in turn affected by these paintings. It is such pictorial transmutations of a single text in the course of time that give to iconographic studies their great interest as a revelation of changing ideas and ways of thought.

For Christian readers a text of the Old Testament may have, as I intimated, a symbolic as well as literal sense—symbolic in that the objects and events referred to literally are themselves signs of other objects, actions, and ideas. The symbolic sense, we assume, was usually, if not always, known to the artist. In his illustration of the written word we can sometimes discern effects of the two great trends in Christian Biblical commentary, the one called the Antiochene approach, which explored the literal meaning in order to make it more fully intelligible in terms of the original Jewish context, and the one developed by the early Alexandrian exegetes, who looked for a specifically Christian theological, mystical, and moral sense as well, a method that is called the "fourfold interpretation."[4] Much in the Old Testament, taken literally, was obscure, incredible, even scandalous to Christian faith, though it was the word of God; and one had therefore to search for a hidden meaning, deeper and more acceptable, as the pagan Greeks had done with Homer. It should be said that the manifest literal sense, in its fuller detail, is often more than the plain historical fact of an episode in the Jewish past. Reading the account of Abraham's Sacrifice of Isaac, we are made aware of an ethical problem and a weighty burden of religious meaning apart from the view of the story as prospectively Christian through the analogy to the sacrifice of Christ.

Another aspect of the illustration of literal meaning is noteworthy in medieval art: the habit of representing the metaphors in the text as if they were simply descriptive terms. When the great artist who illustrated the 9th-century Latin psalter in Utrecht came to the passage in Psalm 43 (44): "Awake, why sleepest thou, O Lord," he drew the figure of God lying in bed and awakened by angels (FIG. 1). At the same time this artist introduced in other illustrations of the psalter various episodes from the Gospels as allusions manifest to him in the psalmist's words. So for the passage in Psalm 86 (87), verse 5: "and of Zion it shall be said, 'This and that

17

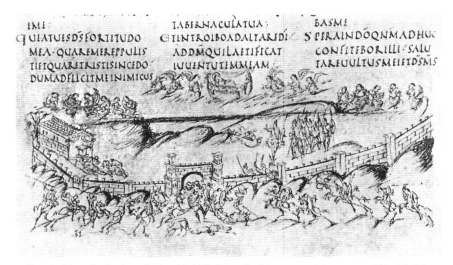

FIG. 1. Utrecht Psalter, Psalm 43 (44), Utrecht University Library ms. 484, fol. 25.

man was born in her and the highest himself shall establish her,'"
he drew a picture of the birth of Christ.[5] He could have approached
Psalm 43 (44) in the same allegorizing spirit, like the Byzantine
artists who illustrated that verse by alluding to the Resurrection
through an apposite image of the Marys at the Tomb.[6] The freedom of interpretation in the Utrecht Psalter, with the frequent
shift from the literal to the symbolic, while the style of drawing and
composition remains the same, is a characteristic feature of this
remarkable book.[7]

In certain works the commentator's allegory is made visible
through the coupling of the literal illustration with a second picture that represents the symbolic meaning. So at an early period a
picture of the Sacrifice of Isaac was paired with a picture of the
Crucifixion, and Isaac Carrying the Faggots with Christ Carrying
the Cross. The pages from a Moralized Bible of the 13th century
reproduced here are examples of this method (FIGS. 2, 3). Yet it
must be obvious that even without the concordant image, a picture of Abraham's Sacrifice could be seen as an antetype of the
Crucifixion. Sometimes the context, the place of this Old
Testament scene in a Gospel manuscript or on a cross or altar,
would be enough to turn the viewer's mind to Christ. Or this connection could be intimated in a more subtly allusive manner
through a single detail: the position of the ram in the bush, suspended by its horns, or the rendering of the bush as a tall plant
with two crossed branches, or the faggots on Isaac's shoulders in
the form of a cross.[8] But where such pictorial cues were lacking, a
pious reader was likely to view the literal illustration according to
one or another of the different senses expounded by the exegetes
and with a focus set by a special interest. For Christians of the

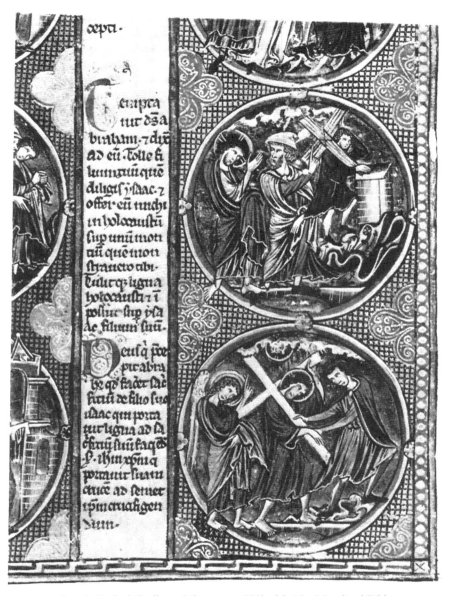

FIG. 2. Oxford, Bodleian Library, ms. 270b, fol. 15v, Moralized Bible.

20

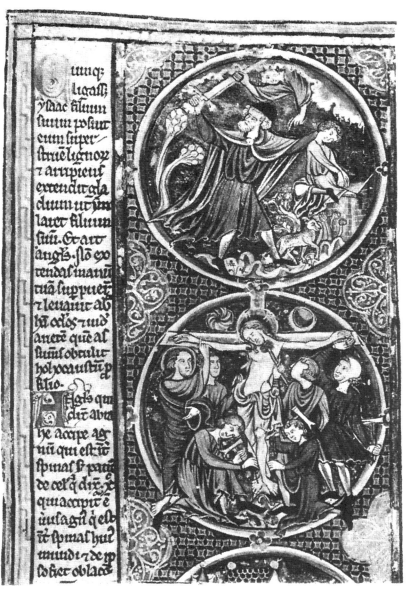

FIG. 3. Oxford, Bodleian Library, ms. 270b, fol. 16, Moralized Bible.

21

early period the Sacrifice of Isaac had been an example of God's help to the soul in danger like Noah in the Flood, Jonah in the whale, Daniel with the lions, and the Hebrew boys in the fiery furnace. It was a promise of salvation through faith and also a model of obedience to God.

But an artist could add a detail or two suggesting ideas that were not part of traditional exegesis and even at times in flagrant deviation from the text. Thus in Souillac in southern France, on the great sculptured pillar of the 12th century, an angel is shown bringing the ram to the Sacrifice, though the Bible speaks of the ram as appearing miraculously in the bush and orthodox commentary made of this miracle a foreshadowing of Christ on the Cross.[9] The introduction of an angel carrying the ram may be explained by the concern of rationalistic commentators with the question of how the ram got to the site of the Sacrifice—a question already answered by Jewish writers who had speculated on the history of this ram and proposed two alternatives: that the ram was created on the sixth day of the world and kept in heaven for this anticipated occasion, or that it was the bellwether of Abraham's flock, brought by the angel Gabriel.[10] In either case the presence of this detail shows that while theologians were occupied mainly with formal and final causes in explaining the great exemplary events in the Old Testament as prefigurements of the New, others, including artists, were interested as well in the immediate efficient cause of the miracle and applied their fantasy to supply the details of such causation, not provided in the Biblical text. But in Souillac this speculative elaboration of the story has been carried much further. On the other side of the pillar are three superposed scenes of a boy fighting with an old man; in the lowest the boy resists, in the second they struggle, at the top the boy submits; but at that point the victorious old man is himself devoured by a monster. One can interpret the series as a free conversion of the theme of Abraham and Isaac into a struggle between a young man and an old, perhaps son and father—a secular parody with a most serious sense. For a modern observer, schooled in the literature of psychoanalysis, these marginal fantasies are also symbolic as projections of feelings about fathers and sons and transpose to the anonymous secular sphere certain thoughts of resistance and struggle aroused by the story of Abraham and Isaac. But an interpreter who proceeded from the conviction that all imagery in the medieval churches is finally part of a coherent system of religious symbolism would be inclined to see the sculptures of the fighting figures as types of evil, of discord and disobedience, contrasted with the ideal relation of Abraham and Isaac, who in a moment of dreadful anxiety and inner conflict experience a happy deliverance.

Chapter 2

THEME OF STATE
AND THEME OF ACTION (I)

To bring out the interplay of text, commentary, symbolism, and style of representation in the word-bound image, I shall consider at greater length a single text and its varying illustrations. It is Exodus 17:9–13, the story of Moses at the battle with the Amalekites, raising his hands to ensure victory:

9. *And Moses said to Joshua: Choose out men for us and go out to fight with Amalek. Tomorrow I will stand on the top of the hill with the rod of God in my hand.*
10. *So Joshua did as Moses had said to him, and fought with Amalek; and Moses, Aaron, and Hur went up to the top of the hill.*
11. *And when Moses held up his hand, Israel prevailed; and when he let down his hand, Amalek prevailed.*
12. *But Moses' hands were heavy. So they took a stone, and put it*

under him, and he sat on it. And Aaron and Hur stayed up his
hands on both sides. And his hands were steady until the going
down of the sun.

13. *And Joshua discomfited Amalek and his people with the edge of*
    the sword.[11]

For the early Christians this episode was an important antetype of salvation through the Cross. It was by assuming the posture of Christ on the Cross and making of himself the sign of the Cross that Moses overcame Amalek. His general and successor is called Joshua, the Hebrew name of Jesus (Yeshua), which means "victory."[12] The author of the Epistle of Barnabas[13] and the early Apologists, Justin,[14] Tertullian,[15] Origen,[16] and Cyprian,[17] all interpreted the story as a foreshadowing of the Cross.[18] It was one of the main examples of their reading of the Old Testament as a prefigurement of the New. A medieval poet, Adam of St. Victor, paraphrasing Hebrews 10:10, expressed the principle concisely: *Lex est umbra futurorum.* The Old Law is the shadow of things to come. Jewish commentary earlier had found a spiritual symbolism in this story of a battle won through Moses' raised hands: when we look upward to God, away from earthly things, we prevail; when we look downward, we are lost.[19] But the prospective method applied by the church fathers was already clear in the Gospels. Speaking to the pilgrims on the way to Emmaus, Jesus, "beginning at Moses and all the prophets, expounded to them in all the scriptures the things concerning himself" (Luke 24:27). Earlier he said to the Jews: "For had ye believed Moses, ye would have believed me, for he wrote of me" (John 5:46, 47); and in foretelling his own death and resurrection he referred to "the sign of the prophet Jonah: 'As Jonah was three days and three nights in the whale's belly, so shall the Son of Man be three days and three nights in the heart of the earth'" (Matthew 12:39, 40).

This reading of the Hebrew Bible as a prefiguration was affirmed by Paul, who saw the crossing of the Red Sea as a baptism and the rock from which Moses brought water for the thirsting Israelites as Christ (I Corinthians 10:1–4). "Now all these things happened to them as examples; and they are written for our admonition upon whom the end of the world is come" (*ibid.*, 10:11).[20]

While an impulse to symbolic interpretation arose in some instances from the need to give to an authoritative but no longer sufficient text a more congenial spiritual sense, the particular prospective symbolism applied here may be traced to Jewish Messianic speculation for which correspondences between past and present, or the past and an awaited future, were signs of a divine plan, a purposive order in history.

The oldest known representation of Moses at the battle with the Amalekites is a mosaic of the 5th century in the nave of Sta. Maria Maggiore in Rome (FIG. 4). Here Moses stands on the hilltop with outstretched hands above the fighting armies. Beside him are Aaron and Hur.

The posture of Moses is like that of many figures in paintings in the catacombs whose gesture has been read as one of prayer; they are called "orants" and represent supposedly the deceased or a personification of the pious soul in heaven (FIG. 5). The same gesture is an attribute of the Old Testament figures already mentioned— Noah, Daniel (FIG. 6), the Hebrew boys, Susanna—who are types of faith and deliverance. It has been asked whether simply prayer is represented by the raised arms, or the sign of the Cross. But for the

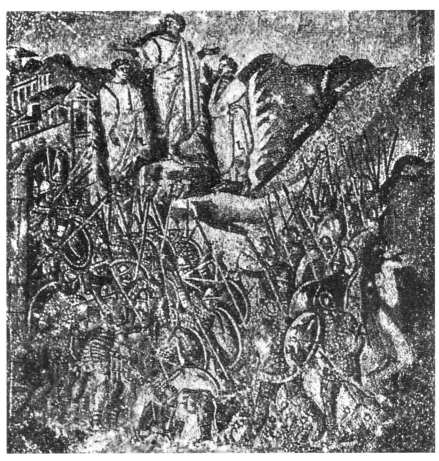

FIG. 4. Rome, Sta. Maria Maggiore, nave mosaic.

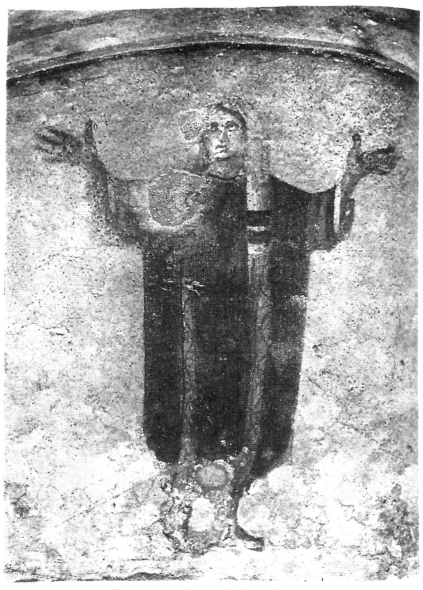

FIG. 5. Rome, Catacomb of Priscilla, Orant.

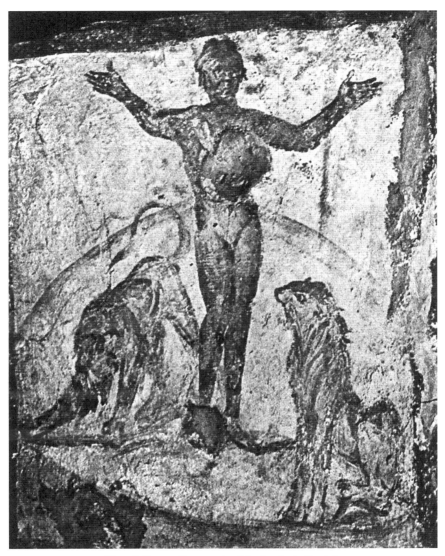

FIG. 6. Rome, Catacomb of the Jordani, Daniel.

early Christians there was no ambiguity here since that posture of prayer with extended arms was regarded as a sign of the Cross.

We note in this first example some differences between image and text. The artist has chosen the moment when Moses' raised arms are not yet weary and require no support from Aaron and Hur. But for this early phase of the battle, the posture is arbitrary with respect to the written words. These state clearly that Moses carried a rod, the same rod with which at God's bidding he divided the Red Sea (Exodus 14:16ff.) and struck the rock in the desert to bring forth water for his people. God said to Moses: "Go on before the people, and take with thee of the elders of Israel, and thy rod, wherewith thou smotest the river, take in thine hand, and go. Behold, I will stand before thee upon the rock in Horeb, and thou shalt smite the rock and there shall come water out of it…" (Exodus 17:5, 6).[21] In the following account of the battle with the Amalekites certain of these phrases recur; even the presence of Aaron and Hur on the hilltop with Moses recalls the elders who accompanied Moses in the previous action.

The text that the artist had been asked to illustrate was a translation that departs in a significant detail from the Hebrew original. In the latter and in the Greek, Latin, and English versions, Moses says that he will stand on the top of the hill and hold the rod of God in his hand (Exodus 17:9). In the King James translation, as in the Hebrew text, Moses at first raises a single hand (17:11); only in the next sentence is there a change to hands in the plural. But in Jerome's Latin version, as in the Greek Septuagint, both hands are raised from the start—*eum levaret manus*—and this reading is followed by the Douay translators.[22] Finally in 17:12 the Hebrew text and all the versions speak of

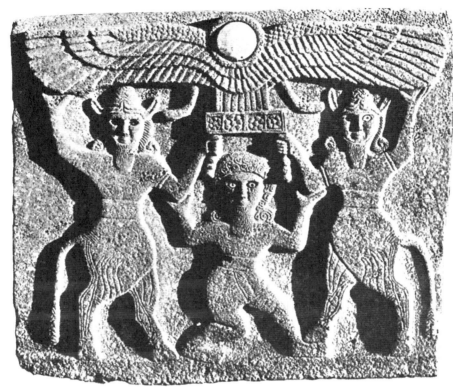

FIG. 7. Tell Halaf, Hittite relief.

both hands as held up by Aaron and Hur, who have put a stone under Moses for him to sit on.

Although the shift in the Hebrew text from the singular to the plural of "hand" seems a contradiction, the plural may be explained as describing the hands raised singly in alternation. When Moses raised one hand and it got tired, he raised the other, and eventually Aaron and Hur sustained both hands while Moses sat on a stone.

Yet one may suppose that the singular of "hand" in 17:11 refers to the raised hand holding the rod which is the source of Moses' strength and has been effective in dividing the Red Sea (14:16ff.)[23] and in striking water from the rock (17:5–7). In the Book of Joshua a similar gesture ensures victory in the battle against Ai. The Lord commanded Joshua: "Stretch out the spear that is in thy hand toward Ai: for I will give it into thy hand. And Joshua stretched out the spear that he had in his hand toward the city.... Joshua drew not his hand back, wherewith he stretched out the spear, until he had utterly destroyed all the inhabitants of Ai" (Joshua 8:18, 26). In the account of Moses the plural form in the Greek and Latin versions of Exodus 17:11 was perhaps read back by the translators from the next line concerning Aaron's and Hur's support. But in the Hebrew text itself two different symbols of force might have been conflated: the raised hand of a victor, like the hand of God, and the king or god with raised hands supported by his attendants or priests.[24] Both conceptions are found in ancient relief sculptures in the Biblical lands (Fig. 7).[25] The raised right hand is a frequent attribute of power which was transferred from the God of the Hebrew Bible and from images of the pagan divinities and rulers to representations of Christ.[26]

In the Christian world the story of Moses' raised arms was an impressive example of the efficacy of prayer in war and through this sense became a model in actual combat. Many accounts from the Middle Ages tell of a ruler or priest who in the midst of battle remembered this story of Moses and assumed his posture.

Eddi Stephen, the biographer of Bishop Wilfrid of York, reports how during an attack on the Channel coast by pagan enemies in A.D. 666, Wilfrid and his clergy prayed to God. "For as Moses continually called upon the Lord for help, Hur and Aaron raising his hands, while Joshua the son of Nun was fighting against Amalek with the people of God, so this little band of Christians overthrew the fierce and untamed heathen host."[27]

In Ireland where the action of Moses was a constant theme and one likened the national saint, Patrick, to the Jewish leader, there was practiced a type of ascetic prayer, the cross-vigil, in which the monk or hermit held his arms up for long periods in imitation of Moses on the hill. This mode of prayer was ascribed to Saints Columba (Columcille) and Finnian during a battle between two rival Irish armies over possession of a copy of Columba's famous psalter; each saint, like Moses, kept his arms raised in prayer for the victory of his own side.[28]

In 796 Charlemagne wrote to Pope Leo III that while it was the king's task to support the church by arms, "your task, very holy father, consists in seconding the success of our arms by raising your hands to God, like Moses, and imploring him to give the Christian people victory over the enemy of his name."[29]

In the next Germanic dynasty in the 10th century, the emperor Otto I in battle "remembered how the Lord's people had overcome the Amalekites' attack through the prayers of Moses, the servant of God. Accordingly he leaped down from his horse and burst into tearful prayers," kneeling before the nails of the Cross which were fixed on a miracle-working spear.[30]

A little later, around the year 1000, King Robert of France is described by his biographer, Helgaud, as serving God and triumphing over his enemies by virtue of the Holy Spirit, just as Moses, the servant of God, won a victory over Amalek by praying humbly with his arms outstretched.[31]

In the First Crusade the animating role of the church inspired what may be taken as the classic statement of this likeness of contemporary and Biblical wars. Pope Urban in his speech at Clermont in 1095 proclaimed to the soldiers: "You who are to go shall have us praying for you; we shall have you fighting for God's people. It is our duty to pray, yours to fight against the Amalekites. With Moses we shall extend unwearied hands in prayer to heaven, while you go forth and brandish the sword, like dauntless warriors, against Amalek."[32]

In these accounts it is sometimes a priest who reenacts the role of Moses, sometimes a king. Yet few of the texts allude to the symbolism of the Cross in Moses' posture of prayer, though the extension of the arms is cited. The literal sense of the few words in the Bible—literal as understood by the men of the Middle Ages—was enough ground for their application to a present combat in which prayer could bring victory. And even apart from the connection with prayer, the raised arm had its own magical and poetic force as "the upper hand" in a battle.

By the time of Pope Urban's speech the picture of the episode had changed in an important respect. From the 9th century onward we see the arms of Moses held up by Aaron and Hur. The

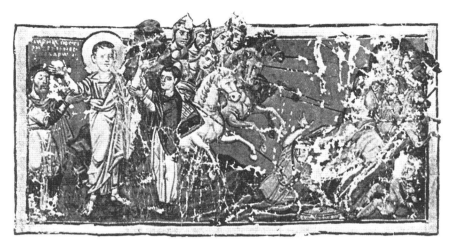

FIG. 8 . Paris, Bibliothèque Nationale, ms. grec. 510, fol. 424v,
Homilies of Gregory Nazianzen.

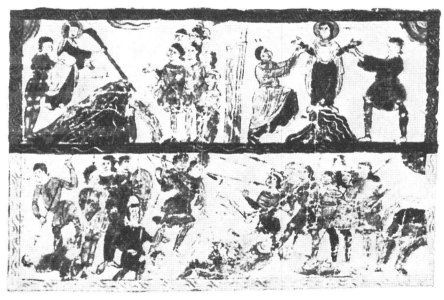

FIG. 9. Vatican Library, ms. lat. 5729, Farfa Bible, fol. 1.

oldest example of this type, preserved in a Greek manuscript of the *Homilies* of Gregory Nazianzen, dated about 880, probably goes back to an earlier model (FIG. 8).[33] The same conception appears in illustrated Greek Octateuchs of the 11th and 12th centuries which depend on a much older prototype.[34] But no examples of the subject have survived from the mid-5th to the 9th century, and we are unable to say just when the new type was introduced. In the Gregory manuscript the image of Moses, Aaron, and Hur illustrates an allusion to the episode in a sermon that speaks of Moses alone, unaided by his two companions.[35] In the West we find the same motif of the two men sustaining Moses' arms in a Bible of 960 in Leon (fol. 40v), and in the following century in two separate drawings in the Catalonian Bible of Farfa (FIG. 9),[36] and a third in Aelfric's Paraphrase of Exodus in the British Museum.[37] In the latter and in the second of the drawings in the Farfa manuscript we note another feature newly selected from the text: the position of Moses sitting on a stone when Aaron and Hur support his hands (Exodus 17:12). This stone was not just a seat for his weary body, added in a spirit of realism, but was perhaps understood in the Middle Ages as a seat of honor, a throne, that served as a sign of his theocratic power.[38] In the Vulgate, a few lines beyond (17:16), Moses recalls God's promise that he will destroy Amalek "by the hand of the throne of the Lord."[39]

There is in Western art since the 11th century, with the emergence of the so-called Romanesque style, a notable trend to fuller illustration of a narrative text. But the motif of the supported arms precedes that trend: and occurring as it does in both Byzantine and Western art, it also invites the question of possible dependence in the West on Greek examples—though, given the common text, an independent choice of the same detail is conceivable in West and East. One can readily imagine that a reader of the text, inclined to the dramatic in the narrative, was impressed by the second stage of the battle, when the leader's arms became weary and had to be held up by others. As a turn of fortune and its reversal through a new action, this moment of the story has an evident appeal and might have inspired the variant image without a prompting of the artist by an ideological interest. I have made the experiment of reading the text to two children aged nine and seven, whom I asked then to draw a picture of the action. Both showed Moses supported; but while the younger represented the two helpers sustaining Moses' arms together, the older boy had only one hold up an arm of Moses while the second stood by inactive. Perhaps he wished the role of supporter for himself alone or, identifying himself with Moses, he imagined a single support—his brother.

I do not believe that in the Middle Ages a traditional picture rendering a sacred text could be changed so readily after a fresh scrutiny of the words. What we wish to understand is the creation of a new type that was widely accepted and replaced an older standard image. If in a modern child's attraction by the idea of the supported arms there may be a psychological pattern arising from needs of the child within the context of his family life and the enjoyment of an imagined role through the story, a corresponding concept latent in a medieval artist had to contend with the authority of an existing model. Yet we know from the history of many such images that compulsion by the model is not so strong as to preclude individual revisions which are then maintained by a new common interest or viewpoint.

For the character of the earliest image of the story, known through the unique example in Sta. Maria Maggiore, I venture the following explanation of its disregard of those features of the text that seem to us so obviously dramatic. Moses as a hero was represented there according to the norm of contemporary classic art which supplied the first Christian painters and sculptors with models. A victorious hero then was generally an isolated statuesque figure even in a group composition. To attach to him two other standing figures as supports would have lessened his distinct self-sufficient being. And this classic conception of the hero was all the more appropriate in a Christian art devoted to a symbolic imagery of divine aid; it was not the physical support by Aaron and Hur but God's intervention through Moses that brought victory.

If we look for a conception favorable to that image of a support in a medieval context, we shall find it precisely in a field that has some similarity to the story of Moses, Aaron, and Hur in the battle.

In two pictures of the German king Henry II (1002–14), one in a sacramentary and the other in a pontifical, he is shown with raised arms supported by two native saints in episcopal dress. In the first (Fig. 10) Henry receives his crown from Christ above him and two angels hand him the other insignia of power—the lance and the sword. It is a scene of investiture symbolizing the sacred authority of the ruler. A punning inscription refers to Henry as Christ's anointed (*xpictos*).[40] In the second manuscript the heavenly figures are lacking (Fig. 11), but there is the same analogy of the king to Christ through his posture as a cross and to Moses through the supporting bishop-saints.[41] That

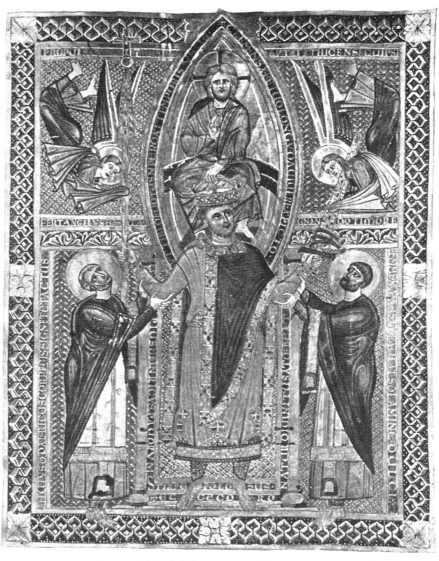

FIG. 10. Munich, Staatsbibliothek lat. ms. 4456, fol. 11, Sacramentary of Henry II.

40

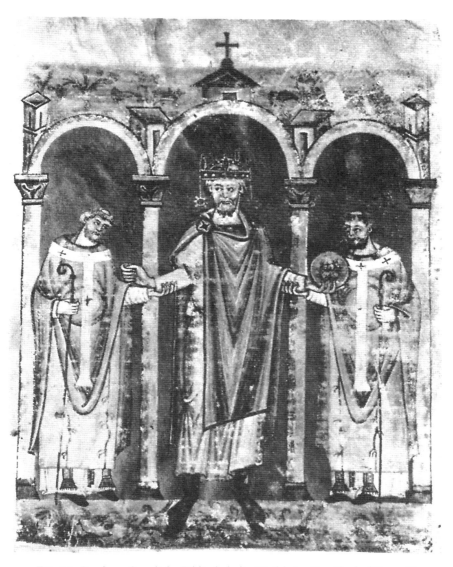

FIG. 11. Bamberg, Staatliche Bibliothek, lit. 53, fol. 2v, Pontifical of Henry II.

41

was how the ruler was conducted into the church on certain feast days and at his coronation.[42]

One may suspect in the likening of Henry to Moses an emulation of the Byzantine monarch, the rival claimant of the Roman imperial crown. Since the time of Constantine the East Roman ruler had been called a second or new Moses. Constantine's victory over Maxentius at the Milvian Bridge was compared by his biographer to the victory of Moses over Pharaoh at the Red Sea; and the miraculous rod through which the Jewish leader had prevailed was preserved in the Byzantine capital in a chapel of the palace and carried as an insigne in imperial ceremonies and processions.[43]

If in the image of Christ crowning the Byzantine emperor, which was the model of the crowning of the Western ruler, the Greek autocrat's arms are not held up by bishop-saints who stand beside him, it may be that his old authority as a "universal bishop" in the Greek Church did not admit so explicit a sign of dependence. In the Venice Psalter of Basil II (976–1025), in the frontispiece showing his consecration by Christ and angels, he stands above eight prostrate figures and is flanked by armed warrior saints who are invoked in battle.[44] In a traditional ceremony the new Byzantine ruler was elevated on a shield by his soldiers, a rite of pagan German and late Roman origin which is represented in Byzantine psalters as an episode in the crowning of David.[45]

In the West the likeness of the ruler to Moses had been spelled out in the eighth century. When Pope Stephen II in 754 found it expedient to invest the Frankish king, Pippin, with a sacred authority through the Old Testament rite of anointing, as a helpful ally and counterforce in checking the advance of the Lombard king in the Papal States, he addressed Pippin as a "new

42

Moses and a new David."[46] In 747 Pope Zacharias had written Pippin that just as Moses prayed while Joshua triumphed in battle, so should the Franks fight while the clergy supported him by prayer and counsel.[47] The authority of Pippin, who, having displaced the legitimate but weak Merovingian ruler, could not claim a hereditary kingship, was strengthened by the sacramental anointing. He was the first Frankish ruler to be consecrated like an Old Testament king; and the papacy in supporting him in this way recalled the precedent of Samuel's dethroning Saul and choosing David.

In these letters and ceremonies, as in the texts cited above, the role of Moses is ascribed at one point to the ruler and at another to the priest. Both are at the same time religious and secular powers in close alliance with each other, an alliance founded on mutual dependence and often disrupted in the following centuries by a conflict of interest. If the image of the archetype priest Aaron, together with his brother-in-law Hur, supporting the arms of Moses in battle could appeal to both the Greek and Latin Churches, its counterpart in the picture of the ruler is known only in the West. The sacredness of the Byzantine emperor and his power in the Greek Church were not subject to the same challenges and strains as the authority of the German emperor in the Roman Church which, while calling on his support, often resisted his claims. It is hard to imagine in Byzantium the complementary symbol of the rulers sustaining the church, as represented in a drawing of the 11th century from Echternach with the crowned Mary-Ecclesia enthroned between the kings David and Solomon, who support her raised arms (FIG. 12).[48]

The image of a royal or sacred personage with arms held up by

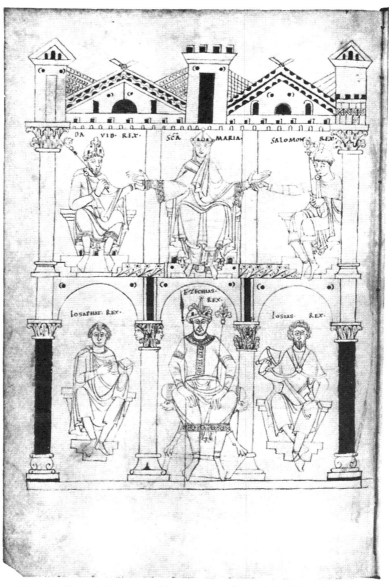

FIG. 12. Paris, Bibliothèque Nationale, ms. lat. 11961, fol. 7, Gospels.

44

other figures may be a sign of power apart from these special relations of medieval priest and king. It may express not a dependence of the supported figure but his power to command support. The scheme of the raised arms, with or without supporting figures, is, I have said, an ancient one in the pre-classic world of the Hittites and Babylonians.[49] It is a widespread form known also in the old African kingdom of Benin where many bronze images have been found of a ruler with raised arms held up by two smaller attendants.[50] Supporting figures in other contexts make visible the majesty of Christ and the power of a bishop. Christ sits or stands in a mandorla held up by two or four angels; sometimes he is shown being lifted up more directly by angels in his Ascension.[51] On a throne in Bari small crouching figures support the bishop's seat.[52]

This old conception of a supported power survived into Italian Renaissance art. Representing Ezekiel's vision of the tetramorph, Raphael placed God in heaven with raised arms held up by two angels. I do not know through what channels Raphael received this extraordinary image. It is not founded on Ezekiel's text.[53]

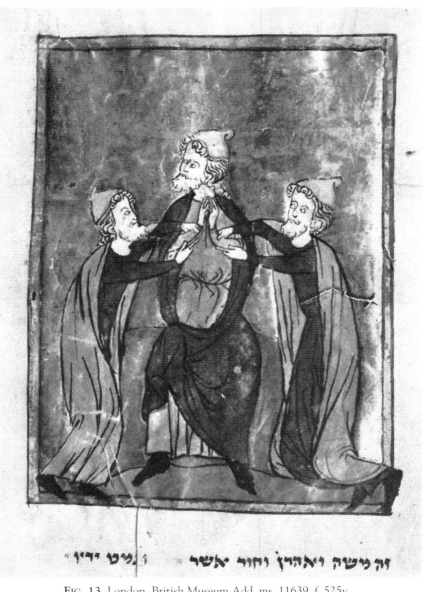

זה משה ואהרן וחור אשר נטל ידיו

FIG. 13. London, British Museum Add. ms. 11639, f. 525v.

Chapter 3

THEME OF STATE AND THEME OF ACTION (II)

If there is a doubt that in the Middle Ages one saw in Moses' raised arms a prefiguration of the Cross—since the analogy is often not explicit in the pictures and the texts—one can point to a negative evidence of this reading of the scene. It is a miniature in a Hebrew manuscript produced in Paris about 1278 (FIG. 13).[54] Here Moses holds both hands close to his breast, a common posture of prayer in Christian art as well. The painter might have been a Christian of the Paris school of miniaturists; but we would suppose then that he followed here the instructions of a Jewish owner of the book. The Hebrew inscription below reads: "This is Moses with Aaron and Hur who support his hands." The illustration of the story, while in accord with the Christian choice of Aaron and Hur—though the battle itself is ignored—was apparently designed to avoid the repugnant symbolism of the outstretched hands. The seated position of

47

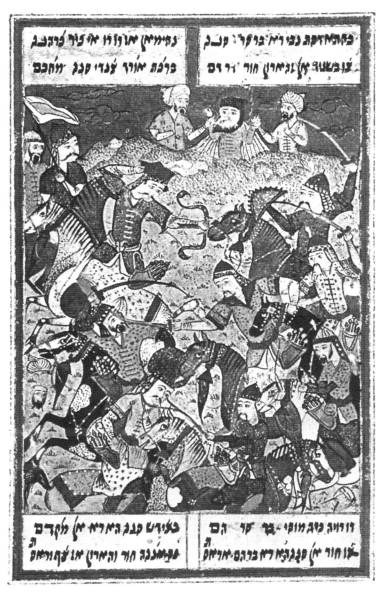

FIG. 14. Berlin, Staatsbibliothek, Judeo-Persian ms. by Shahin.

Moses on the stone is perhaps an expression of Jewish reverence of the leader. But other miniatures in the same manuscript, e.g., the Sacrifice of Isaac, are indistinguishable from examples in Christian painting that follow the literal text and are probably patterned on these models.

The arms raised outward do occur, however, in another Jewish manuscript, a work of the 16th century, in the Berlin Library (FIG. 14).[55] But this miniature, which might have been based on a Christian work, was done in Persia in a Muslim milieu where the symbolism of the Cross was not as disturbing a factor for a Jewish reader of the book.

Students of Jewish commentaries on the Old Testament have noted that certain themes were reinterpreted by the rabbis to preclude a Christian interpretation. During the first centuries A.D., when the Apologists of the new religion spoke of their sect as the "true Israel" (*verus Israel*) and polemicized against Judaism as ignorant and obsolete, the rabbis restated in self-defense the meaning of certain words and episodes of their Bible that were being cited as prophecies and prefigurements of Christ.[56] This process may be observed also in art.

A favored text in Christian polemic against the Jews was chapter 48:13–19 of Genesis describing Jacob's blessing of the sons of Joseph.[57] Joseph placed Manasse, the older son, at Jacob's right hand, and the younger Ephraim at the left; but Jacob crossed his hands in order to give the greater blessing to Ephraim in spite of Joseph's protest. Christian writers found in this episode a prefigurement of the Cross, a meaning reinforced by Jacob's preference for the younger son, Ephraim; the Old Law was replaced by the New, and Ephraim, as the ancestor of the Messiah in Jewish

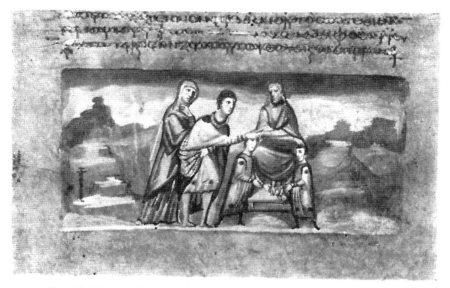

Fig. 15. Vienna, Nationalbibliothek, cod. theol. XXXI, fol. 23. Genesis.

belief, pointed to Christ. In a Greek manuscript of Genesis in Vienna, Jacob's blessing is illustrated by a scene of ritual formality with a prominent crossing of hands (FIG. 15). But in a painting of the same subject in the Dura-Europas synagogue (ca. A.D. 245) the crossing is ignored (FIG. 16).[58]

This reflex of inhibitory interpretation to avoid a distasteful analogy may be found also in Christian art. When illustrating the episode of the hanging of the king of Ai, described in the Book of Joshua (8:29), Byzantine artists chose to represent the cross-pattern of the twin-beamed gallows (*epi xylou didymou*) as a stake or *furca* and showed the victim in profile.[59] Pagan opponents of Christianity had mocked the cult of a God crucified like a common criminal. Constantine after his conversion abolished the cross as an instrument of punishment, replacing it by the forked stake.[60] In Jerome's translation of the Book of Joshua there still appears the word *"crux"* (8:29);[61] but Western artists avoid the literal rendering and represent a one-armed gallows,[62] even in the rare instance where the deposition of the king's corpse is likened to the Deposition of Christ.[63]

For the reader who has followed the account to this point and kept in mind the analogy of Moses to Christ, it will be a surprise to see the miniature painting of our scene in a psalter of Louis IX (Paris, Bibliothèque Nationale, ms. lat. 10525), contemporary with the Jewish example (FIG. 17). Here Moses appears in profile kneeling, with hands close together, a posture that is as far from the pattern of the cross as one can imagine. Has the artist deliberately turned away from the symbolism and ignored the long tradition of church commentators? Elsewhere in the book he has represented other praying figures—Samson, David, and Moses at

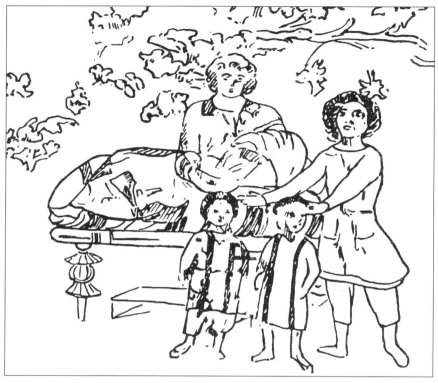

FIG. 16. Dura-Europos, Synagogue, fresco.

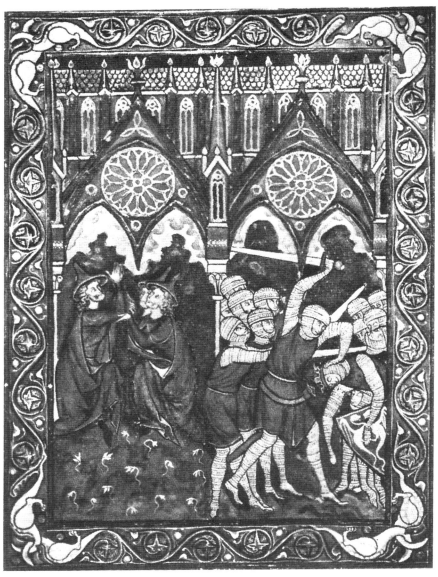

FIG. 17. Paris, Bibliothèque Nationale, ms. lat. 10525, Moses at battle.

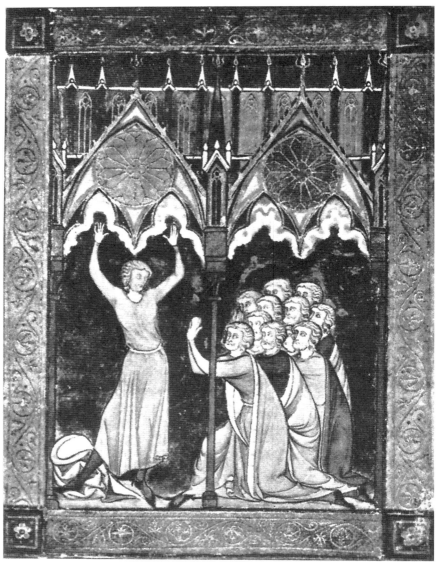

Fig. 18. Paris, Bibliothèque Nationale, ms. lat. 10525,
Joseph revealing himself to his brothers.

the Burning Bush—in the same realistic manner, kneeling and in profile.[64] It seems that another pictorial sign for prayer has been applied to Moses, replacing the sign that had been standard in Early Christian art and had served to make more evident the symbolism of the Cross in this scene.

The change from the frontal to the profile position of Moses may be explained by a characteristic of the art of that time: the heightened interest in action, whether in religious or secular scenes, as an objective engagement in which the actors move in a common space of their own and are attentive to each other without confronting the viewer of the image as in a theme of state.

Represented as in the same field with the fighters and turned toward them, Moses appears to take part in the battle. His arms extend toward the soldiers like weapons in the actual combat, and he kneels as in ordinary prayer.

In the older images of Moses his frontal posture and his position between Aaron and Hur isolate him from the battle, in accord with the text which places him on the hilltop, and give him the character of a sacred person in his own higher sphere of being. In the Early Christian and Byzantine examples he recalls the emperor in certain official representations, enthroned ceremonially above a zone of smaller profile figures in homage, games, or combat.

Though the artist of the psalter favors the profile—whether a strict or a near-profile—as more suited to action, he has not given up entirely the frontal pose with raised hands. But in a remarkable picture where he does use it—the scene of Joseph disclosing himself to his brothers—this posture too belongs to action (Fig. 18). In a subtle way it is both acting in the theatrical sense and an act of self-revelation. Joseph throws off his robes of office and stands

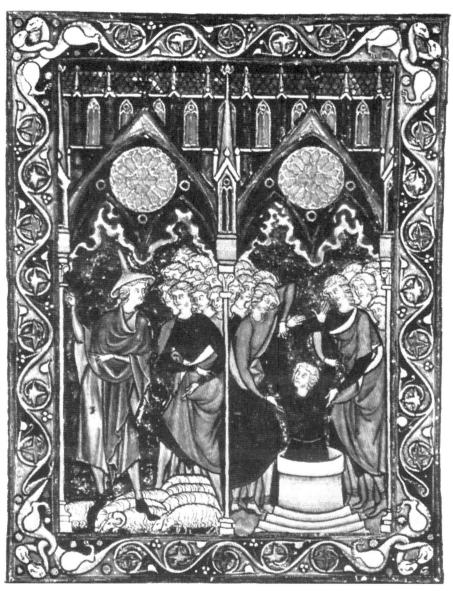

FIG. 19. Paris, Bibliothèque Nationale, ms. lat. 10525, Joseph lowered into well.

up, raising his arms high. Doing so, he recalls to the others his posture when they had last known him as their brother—earlier in the same book the artist represented Joseph being lowered into the well, with his arms raised high (FIG. 19). There is in this climactic pose a reminder of Christ on the Cross; indeed Joseph betrayed by his brothers and then saving them in Egypt was a striking figure of Christ for the early Church writers as later for Pascal.[65] But the power of the image (FIG. 18) lies rather, I think, in the shock of revelation. The moment of disclosure—a poignant evocation of a past that also foreshadows the Christian future—has been realized through a brilliantly conceived form in which self-reference, remembering, and fateful action are condensed in a single dramatic posture.

From the shift to the profile in the picture of Moses at the battle it does not follow that the old symbolic meaning had disappeared altogether. In the 13th century many viewers of this profile image of Moses, with arms held up by Aaron and Hur, might still recall the Christian sense of the episode, just as a picture of Abraham's Sacrifice could awaken an idea of the Crucifixion though the picture contained no element patterned like the Cross.

But there is reason to think that by this time the symbolic sense of Moses' prayer had indeed changed. In the illustration of the scene in the Moralized Bible of ca. 1245 (FIG. 20) a new meaning is made as explicit as one could wish.

Before I describe the miniature I should like to say more about the character of this extraordinary volume.[66] It is an immense picture book where each historical scene of the Old Testament is accompanied by a second picture that conveys the symbolic meaning of the first (FIGS. 2, 3). While ordinarily the pictures in a

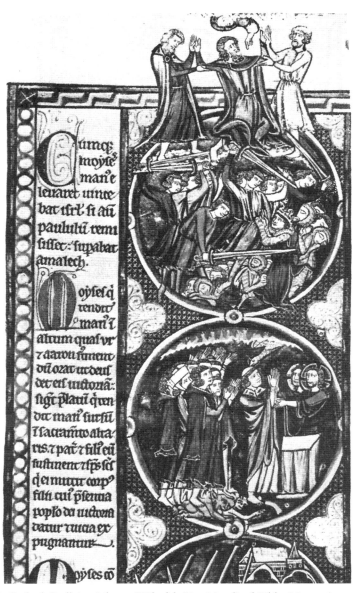

Fig. 20. Oxford, Bodleian Library 270b, fol. 51v, Moralized Bible, Moses, Aaron, Hur.

Bible illustrate the preexisting text, here the written text consists of short inscriptions that describe the paired pictures and explain their connection. These pictures are images of two distinct events or situations, which in turn are understood as the symbol and the symbolized. Although this ordered collection of pictures may be likened to a dictionary where each word is coupled with a defining phrase or with a synonym, the principle of the picture Bible is different. The two images are not substitutable for each other; they are analogous rather than equivalent and the events they depict have an irreversible relation in time. Their analogy points to a divine intention that has determined the two pictured events and their historical connection—a complex causal tie. The first is a sign and preparation of what is to come, as a dark cloud is a sign of rain; but in the scriptural sphere the unique portending events are signs only to a believing reader who knows the unfolding plan of history in which both the portent and its completion issue from God's will.

In the Moralized Bible a scene of ritual follows the picture of Moses: a priest prays at the altar, while figures of God the Father and Christ support his raised hands; with them is a dove representing the Holy Spirit; behind the priest are the laity, all with arms lifted in prayer and all treading on demons.

The inscription of the upper medallion says: "When Moses raised his hands, Israel conquered; when he lowered them a little, Amalek prevailed." The text explaining the second scene reads: "Moses who lifts up his hands which Aaron and Hur support while he prays so that God may give victory signifies the prelate who lifts up his hands high at the sacrament of the altar; the Father and Son support him and the Holy Spirit sends him the body of the

Son by whose presence victory is given to God's people and the vices are defeated."

The sense of the story of Moses has changed from a prefigurement of the Cross to a fore-symbol of the priest at the altar. To be sure, the priest is himself a figure of Christ when he performs the Sacrifice of the Mass. But new here is the specific content of the symbolism of the first scene. A historical episode of the Old Testament signifies now a commonly experienced contemporary event, a recurrent rite, though the artist does not find it inconsistent with this visible actuality of the rite to include in his picture the invisible divine beings named in the words of the Mass and to represent literally as a physical act the metaphor of spiritual support, perhaps to affirm the doctrine of the real presence. The victory over Amalek is likened then to the victory of souls fortified by the Sacrament in their perpetual struggle against sin.

From the prevailing system of scriptural interpretation the author of the Moralized Bible has selected as the essential meaning of the Moses story a liturgical and moral symbolism; but the artist in representing Moses has held to the older analogy to Christ on the Cross.

This pictorial conception of the Biblical episode, with Moses compared to Christ and the whole serving as a symbol of the Sacrifice of the Mass, was perhaps based on an earlier illustration. It had already been expressed in the 12th century by Honorius, an author widely read in his time. Explaining the office of the Mass, he wrote:

In it are represented the sacrifice of the highest pontiff (sc. Christ) and the battle of the King of Glory. Moses prefigured it when he prayed on the mountain with outstretched hands, while Joshua, who is Jesus, fought with Amalek, devastated the kingdom of the defeated enemy, and brought back his people joyous in victory. Thus Christ on the mount of the Cross prayed with outstretched hands for the unbelieving and denying people and, as a victorious leader (dux), fought under the standard of the Cross against Amalek, that is, the devil, and laid waste his conquered kingdom; having defeated the evil enemy, the Lord despoiled Hell.

...Mystery. The bishop images all this and tries to express it in dramatic dress. When he recites the canon with outstretched hands, he represents Christ nailed on the Cross as if he is fighting Amalek, while he simulates Christ's struggle against the devil with the signs of the crosses. Moreover the priests are stationed like the sharp weapons of the fighters, while the deacons are placed behind the bishop and the subdeacons behind the altar.[67]

Note in the Moralized Bible that while the historic priestly group—the praying Moses with Aaron and Hur—is presented as if turned to the viewer in a broadly frontal centralized design and the fighting soldiers below cluster and cross in varied positions ranging from full-face to three-quarters to profile, the medieval priest and his spiritual supports are aligned all in near-profile, as in many pictures of a real church ceremony in that period. The unique frontality and symmetry of Moses is an artistic mode of presenting a transcendent figure or sacred theme of state; the repeated profile of the symbolized content is that of an ongoing action of which the ordered ritual character is marked by its difference from the spontaneity and chaos of the battle. Full-face and profile, though less strict than in some earlier works, function here as contrasted forms of the symbol and the symbolized. Even God the Father and Christ, who are so often shown frontally to convey their sacred unconditioned being, appear in the same empirical profile as the worshipers and the priest. The text of Honorius speaks three times of the outstretched hands of Moses, Christ, and the bishop as a pattern of the Cross; but in the Moralized Bible the empirical mode of representation is stronger than the word and in the picture of the symbolized action the artist has replaced the significant symbolic posture by the less evocative profile of figures in a transient action. And one will observe that even in the upper medallion Moses' figure is less pronounced as a cross than in some older images.

We have seen that in the 13th century, not long after the Moralized Bible was made, another French artist, representing the story of Moses by itself without indicating the symbolic sense through metaphoric detail or an accompanying explanatory miniature or inscription, drew Moses in profile. Here the analogy to the Cross may be implied but is not manifest. The symbolic content of the episode was no longer expressed in the form of the represented posture.

Was the shift to the profile in that picture of Moses a deliberate detheologizing of the story? If the frontal form with its symmetrical cross pattern brought out the Christian sense by analogy, did the profile by contrast convey an idea of the historic event in its concrete actuality? Or, without ascribing to the artist so definite an aim in a particular work, was the change from the frontal to the profile Moses an instance of a more general change from the providential Christian view to the plainly empirical in the imaging of historical scenes of the Old Testament that had once been grasped as symbols of the New?

From later pictures it is clear that the role of Moses at the battle had come to be seen as a minor detail of the action, though
perhaps retaining its Christian connotation for some viewers. In a
woodcut in the Lübeck Bible of 1494 Moses kneels and prays in
profile, while Aaron and Hur support his arms; the three are at
the side of the picture while the battling armies fill the greater
part of the space (FIG. 21).[68] This is how the scene is often represented in Bibles of the 17th century as well.[69] Sometimes the praying group is set far off in the landscape and diminished in size by
the perspective.[70]

An exceptional image of about 1300 on a decorated tile from
the pavement of St. Nicaise in Reims shows how far one had
moved from a symbolic rendering of the story (FIG. 22).[71] Moses
appears with his left arm raised; his two companions help to support it. The artist, we may suppose, had responded to the Hebrew
text which tells of Moses raising a single arm. Here the newly
marked literal detail is a significant selection; one chose the hith-
erto ignored moment in which the leader's raised arm works as a
magic force like Jehovah's "mighty hand." [72]

How much the symbolism of the Cross in this scene had
declined in importance we may judge also from an illustration of
the battle in a magnificent royal picture book of the Old
Testament produced in Paris about 1250 and now in the Morgan
Library. It is one of the fullest series of such pictures, yet the battle of Joshua's army and the Amalekites is represented there without Moses.[73] The painter's chief interest is in the world of combat;
the Old Testament is for him a secular history with memorable
tales of war, adventure, and love.

Throughout the Middle Ages the narrative books of the Old

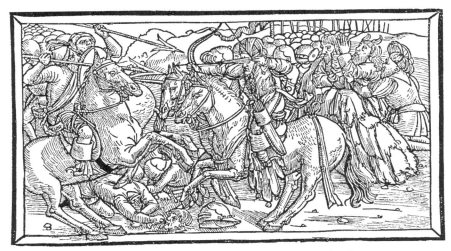

FIG. 21. Lübeck Bible, woodcut, 1494, Moses at battle.

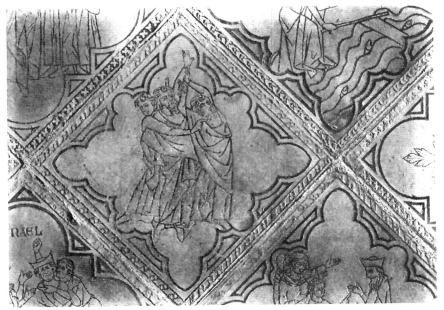

FIG. 22. Reims, St. Remi, floor tile from St. Nicaise, Moses, Aaron, and Hur.

Testament had been read from a lay point of view as an epic of Jewish heroes and heroines, ideal in courage, wisdom, and beauty. Joshua, Gideon, Samson, Solomon, Judith, and others were often named in courtly literature as noble types beside those of the Greek and Roman world. For feudal imagination the Old Testament had a legendary, even pagan, aspect and its kings were the models of a heroic royalty for which the Gospels could provide no precedent. Episodes of the Jewish Bible were quoted then as history and poetic example without regard to the fourfold interpretation.

As with the story of Moses, the secularizing trend in the illustration of a Biblical narrative text, very strong in the late Middle Ages, may be traced also in pictures of Jacob Blessing the Sons of Joseph. By the 16th century this episode, which for medieval religious thought was so highly charged with allusions to Christ and the church, could be represented in complete abstraction from orthodox commentary. I show a woodcut from a Latin Bible published in Paris in 1560 (after a woodcut by Holbein) where neither the crossing of Jacob's hands nor the choice of the younger son for the primary blessing has been rendered, although these details are explicit in the text (FIG. 23).[74]

Even Rembrandt, a deeper artist who was a close reader of the Bible and surely grasped the spiritual complexity of the story, ignored the Christian sense in his painting of the subject (FIG. 24). Placing the emotional content, the grandfather's tender love of the child, above theology and the physical details of the rite, he omitted the crossing of the hands; only one hand is clearly shown and its gesture of blessing is in profile.

As more naturalistic styles prevailed in art, the prefigurative interpretations of a narrative, transmitted by the later exegetes,

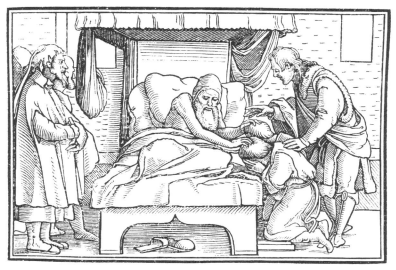

FIG. 23. Latin Bible of 1560, woodcut, after Holbein, Jacob blessing the sons of Joseph.

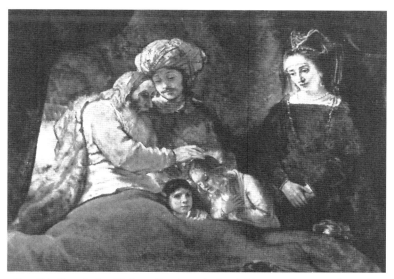

FIG. 24. Kassel, Art Gallery, Rembrandt, Jacob blessing the sons of Joseph.

became less cogent, though they retained their appeal in liturgical contexts and in didactic art. The religious too sometimes spoke of them as curiosities of an affected, outmoded reading of the sacred book. One could excuse them as a kind of poetizing, a search for analogies pleasing to the imagination; but they were hardly satisfying to common sense or reason when presented as insights into a divine plan underlying the historical events.

Early in the 13th century a philosopher-theologian and archbishop of Paris, William of Auvergne, questioned the practice of interpreting the Old Testament as a prefigurement of the New. He accepted the analogies as descriptive or metaphorical, not explanatory. An expositor could make use of one event as a simile to describe another which it resembled in form: but the resemblance did not signify a connection of cause or purpose between the two events.[75]

It is as such a poetic analogy that the story of Moses, Aaron, and Hur has reappeared in our own time, and in a most unlikely place. The biologist Peter B. Medawar, writing on logical syntax and semantics in a "Note on Scientific Method" in his book, *The Uniqueness of the Individual*, says: "A scientific theory is propped up on either side, like Moses' arms before the Amalekites, by twin supports that together form its 'metatheory,' and without these Reason cannot prevail."[76]

Chapter 4

FRONTAL AND PROFILE AS SYMBOLIC FORMS

I shall discuss further in this last part the role of the style of representation in the form of the symbol, and more specifically the frontal and profile positions.

Meaning and artistic form are not easily separated in representations; some forms that appear to be conventions of a local or period style are not only aesthetic choices but are perceived as attributes of the represented objects. What is called frontality may be one of several natural appearances favored in a given style, all rendered with the same kind of line and modeling; or it may be a dominant and even exclusive posture, applied to figures with different meaning, and by its distinctive qualities and accord with other features of the work it may stand out as a pronounced characteristic of the style. The same alternatives hold for the profile position.

The frontality, symmetry, and central place of Moses in some of our examples belong to life as well as art. We know them as

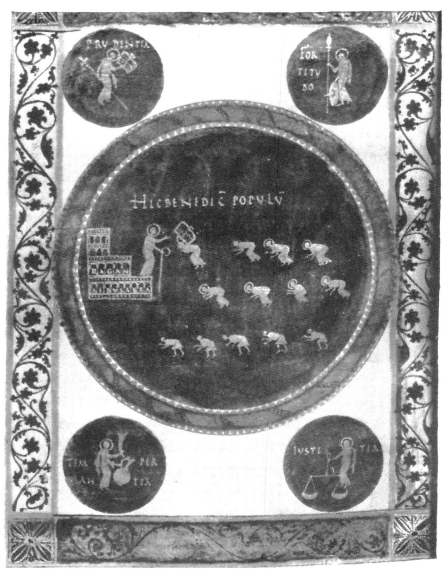

FIG. 25. Autun, Bibl. Municipale, ms. 19bis, Sacramentary of Marmoutier.

features of ritual, a domain of the real in which every detail is a sign. Once they have been established, the dramatic and voiced forms of liturgy created for invocation and reminder of the sacred undergo little change, while furniture, vessels, and vestments are continually redesigned to satisfy a new taste in art. But pictures of the same ritual vary from age to age and show the influence of a style of art. In a style committed to a clear view of the figures in a scene with little or no spatial depth, the painter will not show a rite in perspective as beheld from the nave. He is more likely to represent priest and worshipers aligned in profile.[77] Yet the same artist, to exhibit the clergy as a hierarchy, will choose another arrangement more suited to the expression of rank. An instructive example of the different approaches are two miniatures in the Sacramentary of Marmoutier, a Carolingian manuscript of the school of Tours (FIGS. 25, 26). In the scene of the abbot Raganaldus blessing the monks and laity, all the figures, including the abbot, are in profile; but in the picture representing the hierarchy from bishop to acolyte the differences of rank are made visible through differences of position with respect to the center and through elevation, size, posture, and glance—ranging from the seated bishop, strictly frontal in the center, to the profiles of the lowest and outermost figures.[78]

In medieval art basically different modes of composition co-exist within the same personal or collective style, adapted to different types of content, like the modes in music and the genres in poetry. Elements of two such modes may be used within a single image to convey a duality of meanings or to mark an important distinction.

The effects of profile and frontal depend also on their relation

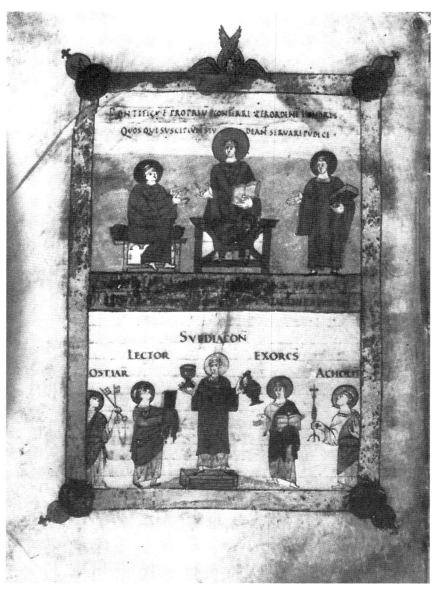

FIG. 26. Autun, Bibl. Municipale, ms. 19bis, Sacramentary of Marmoutier.

to another prevalent type. Since late antiquity and throughout the Middle Ages a schematized three-quarters face was a standard form. It combined aspects of the full-face and profile, independent of an explicit connection of the eye or hand with a specific object. This generalized posture of the head—a vestige of an advanced naturalistic model inherited from classic art—satisfied the archaic need for distinctness and completeness by showing both eyes clearly and the nose in its characteristic profile, while retaining a suggestion of movement. The dominance of the three-quarters view gave to the exceptional profile or frontal figure the value of the unique or the opposed.

In many pictures of the frontal figure the head is turned slightly; the nature of the contrast of frontal and profile as different relations of a subject to an observer will be most evident through comparison of the profile with the strict full-face as an extreme position. The profile face is detached from the viewer and belongs with the body in action (or in an intransitive state) in a space shared with other profiles on the surface of the image. It is, broadly speaking, like the grammatical form of the third person, the impersonal "he" or "she" with its concordantly inflected verb; while the face turned outward is credited with intentness, a latent or potential glance directed to the observer, and corresponds to the role of "I" in speech, with its complementary "you." It seems to exist both for us and for itself in a space virtually continuous with our own, and is therefore appropriate to the figure as symbol or as carrier of a message. That a figure of Christ holding a book inscribed *Ego sum lux mundi* should be drawn full-face is obvious and natural, since it is addressing the viewer. Yet even when representing a particular individual, whether divine or human, the full-face form, especially of the freestanding, isolated sculpture in the round and of the painted or relief image well above the viewer's eye level, may be of the generalized, the abstract man, outside any context and without the subjectivity implied in a glance. In such figures the eyes are often without a pupil and have been interpreted as expressions of a stage in cultural development before thought had reached a truly reflective self-awareness. The eye without sign of attentiveness seems inactive then like the body as a whole.

Yet we are inclined to see whatever faces us as looking at us, particularly if the image is isolated or in the center of its field, even though the eyes are unmarked by iris and pupil. The frontal eyes in a head represented full-face, on or near our own eye level, hold our gaze and seem to follow us as we move to left or right. This uncanny appearance of the frontal head is the source of medieval texts that speak of an image as miraculously observant and addressing the viewer, or take it as a model of the ubiquitous, all-seeing God.[79] Baudelaire, who knew the sensational recent discoveries of the ancient Oriental temples with their giant sculptures, saw these as symbolic figures that speak to us and penetrate us with their intimate glance:

> La nature est un temple où de vivants piliers
> Laissent parfois sortir de confuses paroles;
> L'homme y passe à travers des forêts de symboles
> Qui l'observent avec des regards familiers.[80]

Besides these qualities of the full-face and profile in art, grounded in the everyday experience of the human presence, one must take into account in the choice of these views and their pairing the artist's requirement of balance, contrast, accent, and variation. The exceptional frontal head in a large series of profiles may be unmarked by other traits that singularize that figure as specially significant. In styles of painting with an advancing observation of nature and a considerable perspective depth the varied directions of the head have also a role in producing an effect of free movement, a fuller possession of the space. But though the choice is less restricted here, the artist gives great weight to the duality of profile and frontal as paired carriers of opposed meanings where such opposition is important, and composes accordingly. In Greek sculpture, in which aesthetic considerations are strong, we often discern this factor of meaning in the choice; in a relief showing an author and his muse, the first is seated in profile and the second stands frontal as if the artist wished to mark different grades of reality in distinguishing a person and a personification. The relative importance of such types of content in the subject matter of art will affect the stylistic norms of bodily direction and the deviations from them.

Returning to our example—Moses at the battle with the Amalekites: we have seen how the artists choose at first a posture of Moses that resembles the symbolized content in form. He stands facing us and his arms are extended like the arms of Christ on the Cross. Later he is turned in profile, the reference to the Cross is thereby blocked or weakened, and Moses becomes a part of the action like the fighting soldiers who are also shown in profile. The contrast between the symbol-laden frontal posture of Moses and the profile of the other figures is abolished by the uniform profile or near-profile of all the actors. The earlier rendering of Moses as if turned toward us and with arms outstretched appears all the more clearly then as a specially accented form suited to the reading of the episode as a symbol. The historical Moses in this version is not only himself a sign but he makes a sign which is addressed to the Christian viewer with his awareness of the Cross; while the later profile pictures an action of which the significance is given in the simple denotation of the words of the Bible and calls for no deeper understanding as a symbol.

In the two Bodleian miniatures (FIG. 20) the contrast of frontal and profile, though less strongly marked than before, is a means of distinguishing a past symbolic event and a present symbolized one, the first a unique historic action and the second a recurrent liturgical performance. I do not mean that all examples of contrasted profile and frontal figures have this function or that a symbolic picture and its represented meaning are commonly distinguished in this way; the duality has been used elsewhere to express different polar ideas. In the Moralized Bible the two postures also correspond to an older and a newer tendency of style, so that one form has a somewhat archaic flavor and the other appears more actual, more modern. In the 12th and 13th centuries we know other examples of the conversion of traditionally frontal figures into profile (or near-profile) ones. The human profile in this art is, in general, the more advanced form and its frequency accords with a trend toward the concrete and active; in older art the frontal form is the more pronounced as a vehicle of the sacred or transcendent.[81] Throughout medieval Christian art it marks what I have called the theme of state and is applied not only in theophanies but to royal persons as well. Even in the later period in images of action a king or spiritually commanding figure is sometimes represented full-face.[82]

In medieval art certain figures were presented either in profile or frontally, and we can gauge through them the different effects of the two views as expressive means. In relief sculptures of the Adoration of the Magi above church doors of the 12th century the Virgin is often enthroned in the center of the field like a cult statue, while the Magi and other figures are set in profile on both sides. A tympanum at Saint-Gilles is an example of this type (FIG. 27). But in some works, as on the delightful portal of Neuilly-en-Donjon in Burgundy (FIG. 27a), the Virgin is off-center and turned to the approaching Magi.[83] She is part of a historic action and not an immobile transcendent figure with a distinct axis of her own. Though the relief at Saint-Gilles is the later work and more developed plastically in the sense of future art, it is the profile solution of the earlier artist that will be followed in paintings of the Virgin and the Magi in the next centuries.

Another and more striking example of the change is the rendering of the story of Daniel in the Lions' Den. In Early Christian art and in the first centuries of the Middle Ages, Daniel is a standing figure, frontal and orant, flanked by two lions. When this quasi-heraldic grouping appears in Spanish Mozarabic art, as in the manuscripts of Beatus on the Apocalypse (which include Jerome's commentary on Daniel), we are inclined to see the symmetrical pattern as the product of a folkloric provincial style that converts scenes of action into static ornamental schemes (FIG. 28). But although the drawing and color are primitive, the artist has been faithful to a statuesque classic prototype; the conception of the whole can be traced to the symmetry of a more richly articulated Greco-Roman art. When the same subject was illustrated by a painter of naturalistic tendency in southern France during

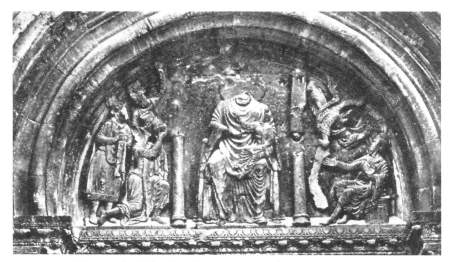

FIG. 27. St-Gilles (Gard), tympanum, Adoration of the Magi.

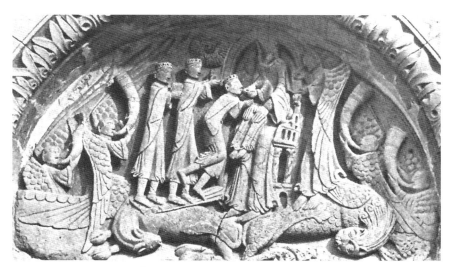

FIG. 27a. Neuilly-en-Donjon, tympanum, Adoration of the Magi.

78

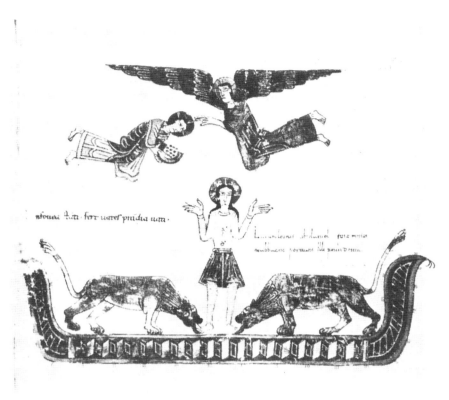

FIG. 28. Gerona, Cathedral Treasure, ms. of Beatus on the Apocalypse, f. 257, Daniel.

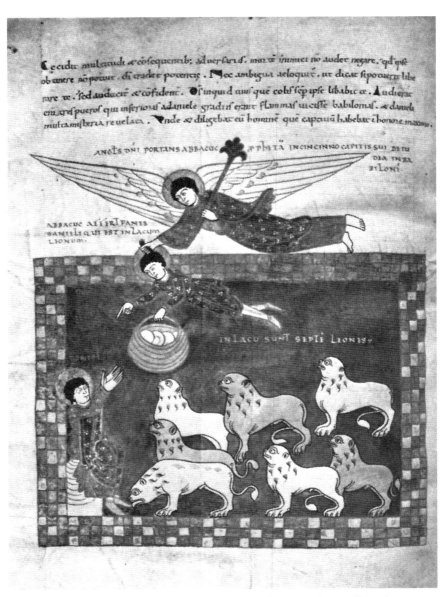

FIG. 29. Paris, Bibliothèque Nationale, ms. lat. 8878, f. 233v, Daniel.

80

the mid-11th century in the Beatus manuscript of Saint-Sever, he gave up the ancient scheme (FIG. 29). He showed Daniel with arms raised in profile as if to receive the food from Habbakuk above him; the gesture of prayer has become ambiguous. Daniel sits at one side in a walled enclosure with seven lions before him in repeated profile. The seated position, new in pictures of the scene, was based on a passage in the Bible (Daniel 14:39) that had been ignored by artists until then, like the reference to seven lions (14:31). The text was read now with more interest in its elements of reality and drama, though the scene retained for the imaginative Christian viewer, even in its episodic form, the old core of symbolism including the eucharistic sense of Habbakuk miraculously transported and bringing bread to Daniel.

These examples and others confirm our belief that the changed illustration of the Moses story is the outcome of more than a change in exegesis. It depends on new norms of representation as well as on a fresh understanding of the text. Though we speak of it as an aesthetic change in style of art, we recognize in it also a change in general outlook and in the attitude to the particular class of objects represented.

A document of the 13th century, in telling of a conservative cleric's resistance to the emerging vogue of the profile, also gives an evidence of the value attached then to the frontal form as both more sacred and more beautiful. A Spanish bishop, Luke of Túy (†1250), condemned as the work of heretics the new one-eyed image of the Virgin. He thought they wished to express their idea of Christ's humility in choosing to be born of so ugly a mother.[84] I can hardly believe that this explanation, which recalls the classic story of Apelles' unusual profile portrait of the one-eyed king Antigonus, presents the true ground of the bishop's feeling.[85] He would not have objected to the rendering of the Magi in profile in a painting or stone relief. More likely what disturbed him was the new style of art in which the Virgin could appear in the same impersonal unmarked profile of narrative action as the lesser figures. We are not surprised to read elsewhere in the bishop's diatribe that he deplored as heretical the new conception of Christ fixed to the Cross with three nails instead of four.[86] He might have seen in the three nails the number of the Trinity, but was repelled by the twisted body, for him an uncustomary and ugly form.

In other arts besides the medieval Christian, profile and frontal are often coupled in the same work as carriers of opposed qualities. One of the pair is the vehicle of the higher value and the other, by contrast, marks the lesser. The opposition is reinforced in turn by differences in size, posture, costume, place, and physiognomy as attributes of the polarized individuals. The duality of the frontal and profile can signify then the distinction between good and evil, the sacred and the less sacred or profane, the heavenly and the earthly, the ruler and the ruled, the noble and the plebeian, the active and the passive, the engaged and the unengaged, the living and the dead, the real person and the image. The matching of these qualities and states with the frontal and profile varies in different cultures, but common is the notion of a polarity expressed through the contrasted positions. Sometimes the body as a whole rather than the face is the carrier of the frontality or profile, sometimes the head more than the body, and there are examples in which the contrast is of profile and three-quarters, of full-face and near-profile, of three-quarters and full-face. The opposition may be of a single figure to a standard pre-sentation of all the others in a group.[87]

In old Egyptian reliefs and paintings where the profile head is the norm for most types of figures, divine and human, the full-face is sometimes given to dancers and musicians and to the dead. Also a minor deity of demonic character, like Bes, is presented full-face. In the system of hieroglyphs the profile head is the sign for "head," the frontal for "face"—a distinction interesting for the role of the eyes in the sense of the body and the self.

A Greek vase painting of dancing Maenads before an image of Dionysus shows the maidens in profile, but the ceremonial fetish of the god frontal (FIG. 30). In another vase painting of a mother with her infant and servant, the latter is frontal, and the mother and child are in profile (FIGS. 31, 32). More often in Greek art the exceptional frontal figure in a relief or painting—the problem changes in sculpture in the round—is an immobile, passive, or constrained person, one that is withdrawn from action.[88] The full-face is also an attribute of the demonic, particularly of the Gorgons. If Dionysus is presented so in the painting described above, it is not only to distinguish the central object of cult most sharply from the celebrants; it is also because the god is simulated through a fetish—an inert mask and robe set on a stick—in con-trast to the living, moving individuals.[89] Where the god himself takes part in an action he is usually drawn in profile. On the pedi-ment in Olympia, Apollo's body in the center of the field is frontal, but his head, in accord with the outstretched right arm that intervenes in the action, is turned in a sharp profile.

In paintings in medieval Arabic manuscripts, which were undoubtedly influenced by Greek tradition, the profile is often

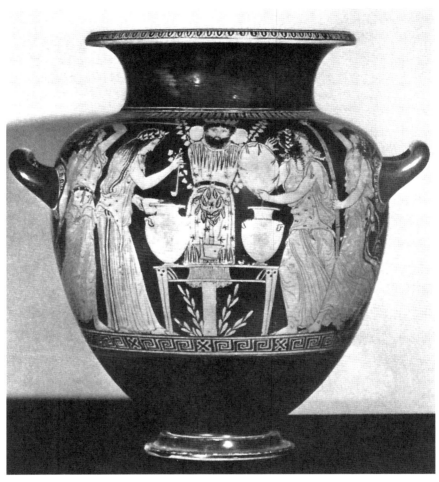

FIG. 30. Naples, Museo Nazionale, Greek vase, Offerings to Dionysus.

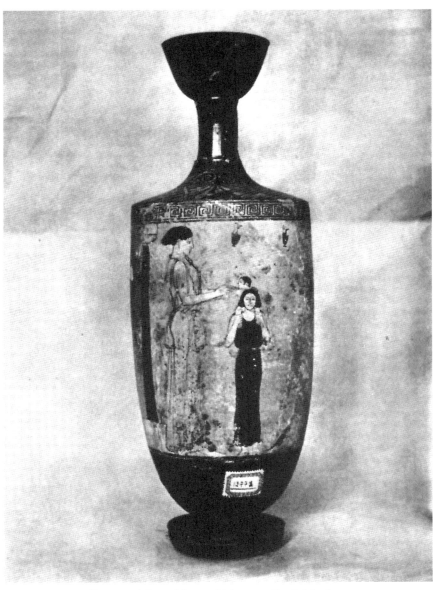

FIG. 31. Athens, National Museum, Greek lekythos.

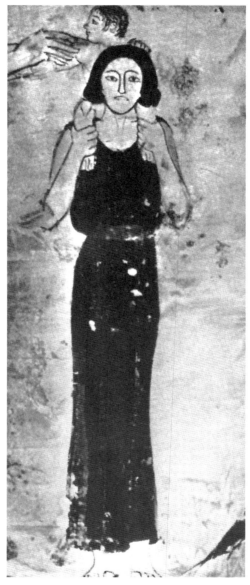

FIG. 32. Athens, National Museum, Greek lekythos, detail.

reserved for the nobler figure in a pair and the lesser or servile one is in a three-quarters view.[90] One may compare the profile here to the deferential use of the third-person pronoun in European speech. But there are enough examples of the opposite choice to show that the contrast as such is more essential than a fixed value of each term in the pair; what counts is the distinction of rank by a different relation to the viewer.[91]

In Western medieval art the profile is attributed to Judas in the Last Supper, in sharp contrast to the apostles and Christ, who are represented in full-face or three-quarters. It is also the appearance of demons in opposition to sacred figures in numerous scenes.[92] But in the same styles the pious donor kneels in profile before a majestically enthroned frontal Christ or Virgin.[93] And Satan as a ruler among his subjects may appear in as strict frontality.[94] In the King Louis IX Psalter (Paris, Bibl. Nat. lat. 10525), where the praying Moses and David are in profile, the evil figures of Ham and Sodomites are also drawn in profile, but in contrast to Noah and Lot who are in three-quarters view.[95] Two senses of the same view may exist then in one style like the variable senses of a word, a grammatical category, or syntactical form in different contexts.[96]

In the choice of profile for demonic and other evil figures one may suppose an aesthetic ground: while the full-face has an ideal closure and roundness—smooth, regular and symmetrical—the profile is indented and asymmetrical and shows a less complete but more sharply characterized face. This was felt by the Spanish bishop who denounced the one-eyed image of the Virgin. The profile was the favored view of the first caricaturists in charging this already broken contour with comic accents and dispropor-tions.[97] But there was perhaps in some uses of the profile in early

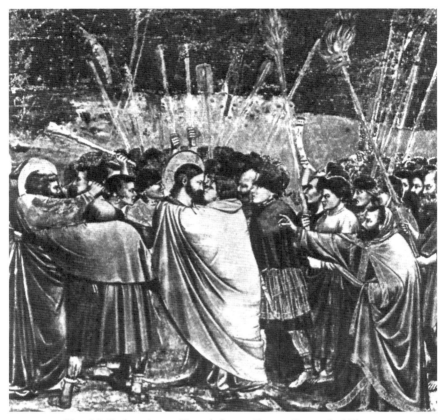

FIG. 33. Padua, Arena Chapel, fresco, Giotto, Betrayal of Christ.

caricature a nuance of detachment that mitigated the affront of pictorial mockery.

Profile and full-face may be regarded as frameworks within which an artist can reinforce a particular quality of the figure through associated features, while exploiting an effect latent in that view. One could also achieve a powerful expression of polar meanings in opposing to each other two profiles with contrasted features and subtly distinguished glances.

So Giotto in representing the Betrayal of Christ as a dramatic actuality, physical and psychic, replaced the old contrast of profile and frontal, traditional in this subject, by a poignant confrontation of two intensely interacting dissimilar profiles (FIGS. 33, 34). A sculptor of the 12th century at Saint-Gilles in Provence had already approached this idea, but merging the tangent profiles of Christ and Judas to form a strange full-face with little sign of feeling, he removed the tension.[98] In Giotto's painting all the figures behind Christ and Judas, except for the profile heads of Peter and Malchus, which reenact with a reduced intensity the opposition of Christ and Judas, are turned toward the center and reinforce the intent glances of the main actors. Only in the narrow space between the profiles of Christ and Judas do we glimpse a frontal face; it is a segment of a face—a nose, eye, and mouth—beside a segment of a profile that overlaps it. Together with the faces of Christ and Judas these interposed heads make a surprising series, a cinematic succession of human features as of a rotating head, passing from the coarse tilted profile of Judas to the noble features of Christ. Giotto's originality of conception will be more evident if we compare his picture with the same scene in the Upper Church at Assisi, painted a generation earlier (FIG. 35). There Christ's

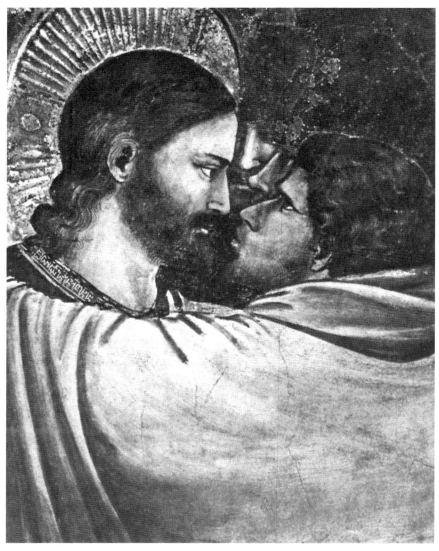

FIG. 34. Padua, Arena Chapel, fresco, Giotto—Christ and Judas.

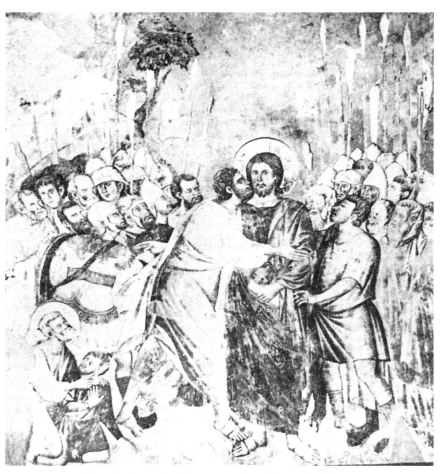

FIG. 35. Assisi, San Francesco, fresco, Betrayal of Christ.

solemn frontal posture detaches him from the profiled Judas and affirms his divine serenity in this turbulent menacing crowd. But the pair lack entirely the inwardness of Giotto's image of the fateful encounter of two men who look into each other's eyes and in that instant reveal their souls. The uncanny power of the glance in a strictly frontal head is transferred to the profile as an objective natural expression, fully motivated in the situation. It is perhaps the first example of a painting in which the reciprocal subjective relations of an I and a You have been made visible through the confrontation of two profiles.

With Giotto in mind one will not take the general shift in art from the stately, often centralized frontal posture to the profile or near-profile of action to be a loss of spiritual depth. Just as a novel written in the third person narrative form can be as revealing of a self as the novel written in the first person which maintains a note of intimate, confiding self-disclosure and brings the narrator close to the reader, so in a painting the profile may carry a subtle expression of a speaking self. The profile portrait, with its more sharply defined and individualized silhouette, has seemed in certain styles and subjects less open to nuances of inner life than the front or three-quarters view.[99] What is specific to the face as a sign of an attentive, responding, or speaking self is not given in every style. As was said before, the full-face is sometimes blind, a schematic mask that is turned toward one but has no penetrating gaze. In many archaic works the frontal stance was only a generalized posture; the artist had yet to discover the fuller range of physiognomic expression in searching both the human face and the resources of his art.

The plurality of meaning in each of these two appearances of the head would seem to exclude a consistent explanation based on inherent qualities of the profile and the frontal or full-face view. It is like the difficulty of finding in colors a universal, culturally unconditioned ground for their symbolic use, though we experience colors as strongly charged with feeling. Both black and white are associated with death, and blue is an attribute of the underworld and of heaven. Traveling through Central Asia, Marco Polo noted that in a province of India black was the preferred color and white was reserved for the devil, while among the Tartars the favored color was white.

The familiar argument from these discrepancies—that color symbolism is entirely conventional—ignores that a color is not a simple elementary feature but a complex of qualities of which certain ones become more or less pronounced in a particular setting and according to a perceiver's experience and attitude.[100] A blue which, as the color of the sky in a painting, looks filmy and soft may appear cold and deep in another painting as the color of hell. Certain of these qualities will be found in other colors as well. Besides, we classify as blue many distinct tones, values, and intensities of blue, with varying modes of appearance; it is a mistake then to look for a unique root affect residing in the common hue. The qualities of appearance depend on physical properties of the individual tones and their obscure physiological effects; but according to the context, which includes the associated meanings as well as the relation to neighboring colors, different qualities or tendencies of a particular blue will be brought into more active play.

So also with black and white, which have striking features in common. Both are achromatic and extremes of brightness, and in these respects are interchangeable as symbols, if what has to be symbolized is an extreme state. Both black and white can convey the void of death. Either can serve as a negation of the vital, the growing, the natural. But the sense of each in a specific context of death is variable; as Plutarch observed in considering different explanations of funerary usage, white clothes are worn by mourners to overcome the blackness of death.[101] By its purity and brightness, white can symbolize the spiritual and innocent; by its lack of color, the inert and cold.[102]

A parallel may be found in the matching of sky and earth or sun and moon with male and female. In Greek and other Western traditions, the sky and sun gods are male and the earth divinity female, as in the gender of words for sky, sun and earth. But in Japan the Shinto ruler of the heavens is a woman. Yet neither choice is entirely arbitrary; we can describe the earth as masculine in its weight, dark soil, and hard rock in contrast to the sky, and the sky as feminine in its lightness, softness, and variability. But one can also proceed from other qualities and match the earth's receptiveness and fertility with the woman, and couple the rain-giving, overarching, sunny sky with man. In both pairings, as in poetic metaphors, real qualities of the symbols and the symbolized are brought out in the contrasted matchings.

Common to these examples of expressive duality is the constraint on matchings inherent in the limited choice. In a representation with a sharply contrasted pair, a quality or meaning of one member as a ground of the image reinforces a pertinent opposed quality in the other. Moses prays while Joshua fights; Moses raising his hands at the battle is the historical antetype of Christ, while the priest at the altar is the living contemporary type. It is especially (though not only) in styles of art with little range of choice—e.g., with a single dominant posture or view of the head, unlike the styles with a richer series of positions—that the extremes of the frontal and the profile can be paired as contrasted signs which accent other oppositions of the two figures. But the use of the polar forms depends also on the weight of the differences they express within a prevailing system of values and on the related frequency of a certain type of theme. We have observed in the later image of Moses praying at the battle how, at a time when the composition of a narrative picture was conceived more and more fully as an objective spectacle in nature detached from the viewer and when the frontal figure became rare or less pronounced in scenes of action, there was an accompanying disregard of the prospective theological meaning. In the 17th century one could easily have rendered the original cross pattern of the praying Moses' raised arms in a foreshortened three-quarters or near-profile view—like the Cross itself in certain pictures with side views of the Crucifixion and of Saint Francis receiving the stigmata. But this was not done. For parallel to the shift from frontality to profile the subject itself had lost much of its force as a Christian typological symbol.

NOTES

[1] I quote this text after Jean Pépin, *Mythe et allégorie* (Paris, 1958), p. 264.

[2] Cf. the example in the recently discovered catacomb in Rome—A. Ferrua, *Le piture della nuova catacomba di via Latina* (Vatican City, 1960), pl. XV, XCI.

[3] See M. Schapiro, "'Cain's Jawbone that Did the First Murder,'" *Art Bulletin* 24 (1942), 205–12.

[4] See Henri de Lubac, *L'exégèse médiévale: Les quatre sens de l'Écriture*, 4 vols. (Paris 1959–63).

[5] See Ernest DeWald, *The Utrecht Psalter* (Princeton, n.d.), pl. 40. To illustrate Psalm 84(85):12—"Truth shall spring out of the earth and righteousness shall look down from heaven," the artist drew the Virgin presenting the Christ Child to a personification of Justice—a woman in the sky receiving the child, Truth (*ibid.* pl. 79, and p. 39 for a corresponding text by Athanasius).

[6] See J. Tikkanen, *Die Psalterillustration im Mittelalter* I (Helsingfors, 1895), p. 63, for examples in the Greek psalters (Chludoff, Barberini, Hamilton) and commentaries.

[7] The artist also elaborates the literal illustration in unexpected ways; e.g., for Psalm 25(26):6—"I will wash my hands in innocency"—he draws nine figures washing their hands in a big basin filled with water from a sculptured lion's mouth at the end of a Roman aqueduct descending from a high mountain, *ibid.*, pl. 23.

Another remarkable Carolingian manuscript with both the literal and allegorical types of illustration is the Stuttgart Psalter; see E. T. DeWald, *The Stuttgart Psalter* (Princeton, 1930), and F. Mütherich, B. Bischoff, B. Fischer *et al.*, *Der Stuttgarter*

Bilderpsalter (Stuttgart, 1968).

⁸ As in the Ingeborg Psalter in Chantilly; F. Deuchler, *Der Ingeborgpsalter* (Berlin, 1967), pl. VII.

⁹ See M. Schapiro, "The Sculptures of Souillac," *Mediaeval Studies in Memory of Arthur Kingsley Porter* (Cambridge, Mass., 1939), 359–87.

¹⁰ See M. Schapiro, "The Angel with the Ram in Abraham's Sacrifice: A Parallel in Western and Islamic Art," *Ars Islamica* 10 (1943), 135–52; and "An Irish-Latin Text on the Angel with the Ram in Abraham's Sacrifice," *Essays in the History of Art Presented to Rudolf Wittkower* (London, 1967), 17–19. In Souillac the faggots carried by Isaac are a rounded bushy bundle of thin branches and could not be taken readily for analogues of the wood of the Cross.

¹¹ I have followed the King James Version, but have modernized the words in a few places.

¹² See T. W. Manson, "The Argument of Prophecy," *Journal of Theological Studies* (1945) 132 ff.

¹³ XII, 2, 3. See *The Apostolic Fathers*, ed. by L. Schopp (New York, 1947).

¹⁴ *Dialogue with Trypho*, ch. 90, 97, 131—Migne, Pat. gr. Vl, cols. 690–91.

¹⁵ *Adversus Judaeos*, III—*Opera IV*, rec. E. F. Leopold (Leipzig, 1841), p. 317. The same text is repeated in *Adversus Marcionem*, III, c. 18, *ibid.*, III, p. 133.

¹⁶ *Homilies on Joshua* cited by Jean Daniélou, *Sacramentum Futuri: Études sur les origines de la typologie biblique* (Paris, 1950), pp. 212–13. See also his *Homilies on Exodus*, XI.

¹⁷ *Testimonia* II, 21—*C.S.E.L., Opera Omnia*, rec. G. Hartel, vol. III, 1, p. 89.

¹⁸ The same idea appears in the writings of Prudentius, *Cathamerinon*, XII; Migne, Pat. lat. LIX, col. 912; Gregory Nazianzen, *Orations*, IV, XIII—Pat. gr. XXXV, cols. 547, 854: Augustine, *De Trinitate*, IV c. 15, Pat. lat. XLII, col. 901; Maximus of Turin, *Homily L: De cruce Domini*, *ibid.*, LVII, cols. 345–46; Ephraém Syrus, *Commentarii in Genesim et Exodum*, ed. R.-M. Tonneau (Louvain, 1965), pp. 126, 127; and others.

¹⁹ Philo, who believed that the literal text, like the letter of the Law, is "a symbol of intellectual things," wrote in his *Allegory of the Laws* (III, 186) that the prayer of Moses with lifted arms "signifies that the soul triumphs when it raises itself above the world of sense" (cited by J. Daniélou, *Sacramentum...*, p. 190, n. 1). A later rabbinical author said: "It was not the uplifted arms of Moses that miraculously made Israel prevail. The Scripture teaches that when the Israelites looked upward and subjected their mind and will to their Father in heaven, they prevailed, and when they did not they fell down slain" (*Mekilta Rosh ha-Shanah* 3:8, quoted from George F. Moore, *Judaism in the First Centuries of the Christian Era* II [Cambridge, Mass., 1927], p. 206). Louis Ginzberg has supposed that the rabbinical interpretation was directed against the Christian reading of

Exodus 17:12 as a prefigurement of the Cross (*The Legends of the Jews* VI, p. 25, n. 145, with references to these and other Jewish texts).

[20] "Haec autem omnia in figura contingebant illis" is the Vulgate text; the Greek version calls these precedents *typoi*. See also Hebrews 10:1, *umbram enim habens lex futurorum bonorum, non ipsam imaginem rerum*. Paul's idea is already in Wisdom 16:6 where the brazen serpent of Num. 21:8 is called "a sign of salvation and a reminder of the commandment of thy law" *(signum salutis ad commemorationem mandatum legis tuae)*. The brazen serpent is cited in the Gospel of John where Jesus says: "And as Moses lifted up the serpent in the desert, so must the Son of Man be lifted up..." (3: 14).

[21] Another discrepancy is the presence of the hand of God in the sky, to which Moses turns his head. God does not address Moses during the battle, but afterward in Exodus 17:14.

[22] The singular form *manum* was not altogether unknown in the Latin world. The editor of Cyprian's *Testimonia* (II, 21—C.S.E.L., rec. G. Hartel [1868], III, 1, p. 89) cites an exceptional manuscript (of the 8th–9th century) with this reading. In the apparatus of variants in the recent Vatican edition of the Latin Bible (ed. H. Quentin) are noted two examples—*sub* Ex. 17:11, 12—in medieval manuscripts.

[23] The Lord says to Moses: "Tu autem eleva virgam tuam, et extende manum tuam super mare, et divide illud."

[24] Cf. Exodus 13:9—God led the Jews out of Egypt *in manu forti*; Ex. 14:9—the Israelites departed from Egypt *in manu excelsa*; Ex. 15:6—Moses' canticle, "Dextera tua, Domine"; and 15:12—"Extendisti manum tuam et devoravit eos terra." For the raised staff or rod as God's hand see Hugo Gressmann, *Mose und sein Zeit* (Göttingen, 1913), pp. 158–59, and in *Die Schriften des alten Testaments* II: *Die Anfänge Israels* (Göttingen, 1922), pp. 101–2.

Perhaps significant for a conflation of older texts in Exodus 17 is the fact that the rod is called *Elohim*'s in 17:9, while the hand is *Yahveh*'s in 17:16.

[25] For a figure with both arms raised, cf. the relief of a winged man with an eagle's head from the city gate of Sendjirli—A. Jeremias, *Das alte Testament im Lichte des alten Orients*, 2nd ed. (Leipzig, 1906), FIG. 201, and a relief from Babylon of a god holding in his raised hands an ax and a whip of lightning, *ibid*. FIG. 44. For the figure (or divine emblem) with raised arms or wings supported by two figures, cf. the relief at *Tell Halaf*— M. von Oppenheim, *Tell Halaf* (London, n.d.), pl. 8b (our FIG. 7), and the examples reproduced by E. Herzfeld, "Die Kunst des zweiten Jahrtausends in Vorderasien," *Archäologische Mitteilungen aus Iran* 9 (1938), 1ff. and FIGS. 124, 132. See also H. P. L'Orange, *Studies in the Iconography of Cosmic Kingship in the Ancient World* (Oslo, 1953), FIGS. 65c, 77. In the Greenfield Papyrus (British Museum) of the Egyptian *Book of the*

Dead (10th century B.C.) the sky goddess Nut is represented as an arched figure supported by the raised arms of Shu (= air) whose own arms are held up by two smaller bull-headed figures (D. Diringer, *The Illuminated Book* [London, 1958], pl. 1, 3b).

²⁶ An early Christian miracle-working mosaic image of Christ in Ravenna, called "Brachium Forte," was invoked in prayer as the same hand that led the children of Israel out of Egypt—Agnellus, *Liber Pontificalis, Vita Neonis*, Pat. lat., CVI, cols. 519–20. For the raised right hand of power in ancient and Christian art, see L'Orange, *Studies in the Iconography...*, pp. 139ff.

²⁷ See B. Colgrave, *Eddius Stephanus Life of Bishop Wilfrid* (Cambridge, 1927), pp. 28–29.

²⁸ See L. Gougaud, *Christianity in Celtic Lands* (London, 1932), pp. 90, 93, 94, 271, 272, 281. The figure with raised arms appears in pagan Celtic art in a context of combat and hunt on the Gundestrup Cauldron and in Scandinavian art on the lost Gallehus Horns. For the latter see W. Hartner, *Die Goldhörner von Gallehus* (Wiesbaden 1969), FIGS. 1, 1a, 3.

²⁹ *Monumenta Germaniae historiae*, Epistolae IV, pp. 137ff. Cf. also Alcuin's letter to Charlemagne in 800 on a victory in war: "For Moses, whom you propose to us as an example after having won the battle and put to flight the Amalekites..." (Pat. lat., C, col. 331, ep. 109); and another letter to Archbishop Paulinus (800) on his fight against heretics: "it is for us to help you, with humble prayers, like Moses with hands raised to heaven," *ibid.*, col. 343 (ep. 113).

³⁰ See Liudprand of Cremona, *Antapodosis*, IV, 24. I quote from *The Works of Liudprand of Cremona* (London, 1930), transl. by F. A. Wright, p. 159.

There is a similar episode in a poem by the deacon Theodosius on the expedition to Crete led by Nicephorus Phocas ca. 960. The king chants Psalm 27: 1 for God's help; "then you, in battle, acted as Moses once did, who defeated Amalek by raising his hands high"—Pat. gr. CXIII, col. 1035.

³¹ See the translation by E. Pognon, *L'an mille* (Paris, 1947), p. 250.

³² It is reported by Balderic of Dol, *Historia Hierosolymitana*, I, 45, translated by A. Krey, *The First Crusade* (Princeton, 1921), p. 36.

There is perhaps an echo of the Crusades in a passage in Alexander Neckam's *De Naturis Rerum*, c. III, following a comment on Ishmael: "Let us pray with Moses, holding up our hands to God, and the true Joshua will fight for us and defeat the Amalekites. Let us then follow the true Joshua as our leader so that the land promised us on high may be allotted to us as the true sons of Israel" (ed. by Thomas Wright [London, 1863], p. 28). For a helpful suggestion in translating this text I wish to thank Professor Harry Caplan of Cornell University.

³³ The inscription refers to "Moses propped up by Aaron and Hur." The miniature is reproduced and described by H. Omont, *Miniatures des plus anciens manuscrits grecs de la Bibliothèque nationale du VIe au XIVe siècle* (Paris, 1929).

³⁴ See D. Hesseling, *Miniatures de L'Octateuque grec de Smyrne* (Leyden, 1909), pl. 61, no. 185; J. Wilpert, *Die römischen Mosaiken und Malereien* I (Freiburg im Breisgau, 1916), Fig. 468 (Vatican Library ms. gr. 746).

³⁵ It is *Oration XIII*, on the consecration of Bishop Eulalios—Pat. gr. XXXV, col. 854—"through the symbolical mystic figure of the hands he [Moses] smashed the Amalekite host. The hands of the priest, lifted up on the mountain and posed in prayer, could accomplish what many thousands of men could not do." See also *Oration IV*, against Julian, for the same thought—*ibid.*, col. 547.

There is a remarkable example in a Greek manuscript of the same period in Smyrna, where a picture of Moses at the battle with the Amalekites, with his hands supported by Aaron and Hur, is juxtaposed to a waterscape with an ibis. The accompanying text of the *Physiologus* describes the ibis (Leviticus 11:17) as a bird that does not know how to dive and lives in shallow waters where the impure fishes abide. The Christian moral: "O man! learn to dive deep so that you may reach the depths of the wisdom and knowledge of God. If you do not stretch out your hand and make the sign of the Cross, you will never sail over the sea of life. To give light, the sun stretches forth its beams, and the moon its horns; and the bird, to fly, stretches out both wings. Moses, when he stretched out his hands, conquered Amalek; so did Daniel subdue the lions." The writer goes on to cite the examples of Jonah, Thekla, Susanna, Judith, Esther, and the Three Boys in the Furnace, all of whom were saved by faith. See J. Strzygowski, *Der Bilderkreis des griechischen Physiologus des Kosmas Indikopleustes und Oktateuch* (Leipzig, 1899), p. 41. The original text of the *Physiologus* is of the Early Christian period and makes no mention of Aaron and Hur, whose presence in the illustration, supporting the arms of Moses, is probably a late addition.

³⁶ On the Farfa Bible, see W. Neuss. *Die Karalanische Bibel illustration* (Bonn, 1922). Figs. 1, 7 (Fig. 1 is mislabeled as of the Roda Bible). See also Fig. 24 for a copy of the second of these miniatures on the 12th-century sculptured portal of Ripoll in Catalonia.

³⁷ British Museum, Cotton Ms. Claudius B IV, f. 95v—Arthur Kingsley Porter believed that Moses, Aaron, and Hur were represented still earlier in the 8th-century Book of Kells on the page (fol. 114) that is usually interpreted as the Arrest of Christ (*The Crosses and Culture of Ireland* [1931], pp. 51–53). His argument that the miniature precedes by two pages the text of the Arrest (Matthew 26:47–50) and therefore cannot be of that subject overlooks the fact that in the early Middle Ages the chapter divisions

were unlike the present ones and that the section with the account of the Arrest began then at 26:30: "Et hymno dicto exierunt in montem Oliveti" (see S. Beissel, *Die Entstehung der Perikopen des römischen Messbuches* [Freiburg im Breisgau, 1907], p. 201), precisely the words inscribed over the Kells miniature. Besides, the subject of Moses has no apparent connection with the text of Matthew 26:30—Christ in Gethsemane. The type of Arrest in the Book of Kells, with two unarmed men seizing Christ by the arms, agrees with several other early examples: the 6th-century Gospels in Cambridge—Corpus Christi College ms 286; an ivory in the Louvre (G. Millet, *Recherches sur l'iconographie de l'évangile* [Paris, 1916], FIG. 333); a Syriac miniature in the British Museum (*ibid.*, FIG. 339), a relief in Raphoe, Ireland (Porter, 1931: FIG. 81), a drawing in the Anglo-Saxon Psalter, British Museum Ms. Tiberius C VI, and sculptures on Irish stone crosses at Armagh, Connor, and Monasterboice (F. Henry, *La sculpture irlandaise* [Paris, 1933]).

[38] In the Aelfric manuscript Moses sits on a slab of yellow stone, and the kneeling Aaron and Hur support his arms in their veiled hands. Rabanus Maurus, in a commentary on Exodus (Pat. lat., CVIII, cols. 84, 85), likens the stone to the Church; Moses sits on the stone "cum lex requievit in Ecclesia."—A Byzantine writer, George Cedrenus, in describing the battle with the Amalekites in his compendium of history, has Aaron and Hur support Moses by placing stones under his hands (Pat. gr. CXXI, col. 170)—perhaps a copyist's defective reading of Cedrenus's text.

[39] "Quia manus solii Domini...erit contra Amalek" (cf. also Exodus 17:14). The Latin is an arbitrary version of the Hebrew text which is itself obscure and perhaps referred simply to the hand holding the rod as the Lord's standard or sign.

[40] On this miniature in Munich Staatsbibliothek lat. 4456, see George Swarzenski, *Die Regensburger Buchmalerei* (Leipzig, 1901), pp. 64–65, 73–74; and P. E. Schramm and F. Mütherich, *Denkmale der deutschen Könige und Kaiser* (Munich, 1962), p. 157, no. 111.

[41] Bamberg, Staatsbibliothek lit. 53, *ibid.*, p. 159, no. 117. See also the *Pericope Book of Henry III* (1039–43) from Echternach for a similar picture of the emperor and his mother, Gisela—Bremen Staatsbibliothek B 21 (*ibid.*, p. 173, no. 153, and A. Goldschmidt, *German Book Illumination* II [New York, n.d.], pl. 53).

[42] See P. E. Schramm, "Das Herrscherbild in der Kunst des frühen Mittelalters," *Vorträge der Bibliothek Warburg* I (1922–23) (1924), p. 210 and notes 216, 221. A similar ceremony is described by Geoffrey of Monmouth in his imaginary account of the coronation of King Arthur—*Historia Regum Britanniae*, IX (ed. by Griscom and Jones, p. 455).

[43] See O. Treitinger, *Die Oströmische Kaiser- und Reichsidee vom Oströmische*

Staats- und Reichsgedanken, 2nd ed. (Darmstadt, 1956), pp. 130ff., 133; and A. Grabar, *L'empereur dans l'art byzantin* (Paris, 1936), pp. 95–97. J. Tikkanen (*Psalterillustration* I [1895], p. 45) notes that in the Byzantine Psalter (British Museum Add. Ms. 19352). Moses' rod at the miracles of the Red Sea and the rock of Horeb is a cross staff and that Byzantine liturgy refers to the rod as a type of the Cross. In the Syriac *Book of the Bee*, the rod is said to be a branch of the tree of knowledge, transmitted to Moses by way of Abraham, Joseph of Nazareth, and Judas Iscariot; it served as the transverse beam of the Cross (M. Grünbaum, *Neue Beiträge zur semitischen Sagenkunde* [Leiden, 1893], pp. 162–63).

[44] Grabar, 1936: pl. XXIII. For the role of prayer and religious rites in Byzantine warfare, see J. R. Vieillefond, "Les pratiques religieuses dans l'armée byzantine d'après les traités militaires," *Revue des Études Anciennes* 37 (1935), 322–30. He cites an anonymous 10th-century Byzantine text on military tactics in which the general charges certain officers to preach to the army, to "proclaim that the victories fulfill the prophecies of the saints and to predict the defeat of the enemy according to the sacred books" (p. 326).

[45] For the texts and images, see L'Orange, 1953: FIGS. 76, 78–80. A parallel to this modeling of the pictures of Old Testament ceremonial on actual state ceremonies of the day, and the variation of those pictures with changes in ideological and political relations of church and state, appear in the conception of images of the Anointing of David by Samuel in medieval art. In Early Christian and Byzantine art David always stands in pictures of this subject. In the West, ever since the anointing and papal crowning of the Carolingian rulers, David often kneels (cf. the miniature in the Stuttgart Psalter); and where he is shown seated on his throne in this scene we suspect sometimes, besides the assimilation to contemporary ceremony, an assertion of the monarch, and in the standing posture a conservative copying of an old Byzantine model. See M. Schapiro, "An Illuminated English Psalter of the 13th Century," *Journal of the Warburg and Courtauld Institutes* 23 (1960), 181ff.

[46] *Mon. Germ. Hist.*, Ep., III, 1, p. 505, no. 11: see also p. 552, no. 39; p. 554, no. 42; and p. 649, no. 98.

[47] *Mon. Germ. Hist.*, pp. 479–80, no. 3. See also ep. no. 33. In a letter to Pippin, addressing him as a "New Moses," Pope Paul I quotes Psalm 88 (89):22: *ecce manus eius auxiliabitur tui, et brachium ipsius confortabit te*, changing the pronouns to shift the reference from David to Pippin—*ibid.*, p. 555.

[48] Cf. the formula of Charlemagne: *Ego Karolus rex et rector regni Francorum et devotus sancti Dei ecclesiae defensor humilisque adiutor*, quoted by P. E. Schramm, *Kaiser, Könige und Päpste* I (Stuttgart, 1968), pp. 184–85. The idea that the royal power is

obligated to aid the church was expressed earlier in a letter of Bede to Bishop Ecgbert, *Opera Historica Bedae*, I, ed. by C. Plummer, p. 412.

⁴⁹ See p. 20 above and n. 25.

⁵⁰ See *Antique Works of Art from Benin*, collected by General Pitt-Rivers (London, 1900), pl. 2, FIG. 7; pl. 12, FIG. 76, etc.

⁵¹ As on the reliefs on the tympana of S. Isidoro in León (A. K. Porter, *Romanesque Sculpture of the Pilgrimage Roads* [Boston, 1923], ill. 702) and St. Sernin in Toulouse (*ibid.*, ill. 308–10). There is a pagan parallel in an ivory carving of the 5th century A.D. with a scene of apotheosis of a ruler who is lifted up by two winged figures (W. F. Volbach, *Elfenbeinarbeiten der Spätantike und des frühen Mittelalters*, 2nd ed. [Mainz, 1952], nr. 56, pl. 14). But a Biblical source may be found in Psalm 90 (91):12—"angels shall bear thee up in their hands." In the Utrecht Psalter, f. 10v, ps. 18 (19), (DeWald, n.d.: pl. XVI), Christ is drawn with arms supported by two angels at the door of the Temple, to illustrate verse 6, "as a bridegroom coming out of his bride chamber." In the Winchester Psalter, British Museum Cotton Ms. Nero C IV, in the scene of the Doubting Thomas (f. 26), two apostles hold up Christ's extended arms.

⁵² See Porter, 1923: ill. 152–55. For a related conception in the old Orient, cf. the throne in the reliefs at Persepolis (L'Orange, 1953: FIGS. 56, 58–60). There may be an echo of this image merged with that of the enthroned Byzantine ruler in a picture and text of the Lapidary of Alfonso X in the Escorial Library. The miniature shows a man, with arms raised, sitting on a four-legged bench held up by four winged men. According to the text the picture represents the power that heaven (Jupiter) will give to one who finds at the astrologically right time the precious stone called *yarganza amariella*. There existed perhaps a gem engraved with such an image of the enthroned ruler. See the facsimile edition: *Lapidario del rey Alfonso X* (Madrid, 1883), fol. 102.

⁵³ It is the painting now in the Pitti Gallery in Florence. The picture was perhaps inspired in part by passages in the Psalms, e.g., 17(18):10—"and he rode upon a cherub, and did fly"; 98(99):1—"he sitteth between the cherubim," which is followed in 98:6 by reference to Moses and Aaron—"They called upon the Lord and he answered them."

⁵⁴ British Museum Add. Ms. 11639, f. 525v. It is a collection of Bible readings, prayers, and other texts. See G. Margoliouth, *Hebrew and Samaritan Manuscripts in the British Museum*, Part III (1915), pp. 402 ff. B. Narkiss (*Hebrew Illuminated Manuscripts* [New York, 1969], p. 86) dates it "c. 1280" and places it in "Troyes (?)."

⁵⁵ The text is of the 14th-century poet Shahin—see the *Encyclopedia Judaica* 9 (Berlin 1939), col. 565, and the frontispiece for a color reproduction of this page. The way of raising the arms, close to the sides of the body, also weakens the analogy to the Cross; but a similar gesture appears in the second drawing of the scene in the Farfa Bible

and is often ascribed to Christ in the Last Judgment where the wounds on the hands are more pointedly exposed in this position. I owe my knowledge of the Shahin miniature to the kindness of Professor Rachel Wischnitzer.

[56] See Louis Ginzberg, *The Legends of the Jews* in note 19; also Marcel Simon, *Verus Israel: Études sur les relations entre Chrétiens et Juifs dans l'Empire Romain* (135–425) (Paris, 1948).

[57] Simon, 1948: 191.

[58] See Carl Kraeling, The *Synagogue* (*The Excavations at Dura-Europos,* VIII, 1; *Final Report*) (New Haven, 1956), FIG. 58, p. 222. The crossing of the hands is clearly marked in the 4th-century painting in the recently discovered catacomb of the Via Latina in Rome; A. Ferrua, *Le pittore della nuova catacomba di via Latina* (Vatican City, 1960), pl. XXV.

[59] See *Il Rotulo di Giosué Codice Vaticano Palatino Greco* 431 (Milan, 1905), pl. 13, 14, 19; K. Weitzmann, *The Joshua Roll* (Princeton, 1948), pl. IV, FIG. 34; pl. XIII, FIG. 46; A. Goldschmidt and K. Weitzmann, *Die byzantinischen Elfenbeinskulpturen des X–XIII Jahrhunderts* (Berlin, 1930), pl. 1, 2; S. Cirac Estopañan, *Skyllitzes Matritensis*, I; *Reproducciones y Miniaturas* (Barcelona-Madrid, 1965), f. 98v, no. 228—for a later hanging on a forked stake.

[60] Th. Mommsen, *Römisches Strafrecht* (Leipzig, 1899), p. 921.

[61] "...deposuerunt cadaver eius de cruce."

[62] Cf. the Moralized Bible, Bodleian ms. 270b, f. 99v, where the king of Ai hangs by the neck from a gallows beam set in a forked stake. It is coupled with a scene of Christ on the Cross, but the text speaks of the victory of the spiritual over the wicked through Christ's Crucifixion; Joshua stands with raised shield (as in 8:18, 19—a mistranslation of the Hebrew for spear) beside the hanging king.

[63] As on the Klosterneuburg Altar; F. Rohrig, *Der Verduner Altar* (Vienna, 1955), pl. 31. These two plaques do not belong to the original work of 1181 by Nicholas of Verdun but were added in the early 14th century. In the Morgan Library Picture Bible of the 13th century (see the new edition, *Old Testament Miniatures*, with text by S. Cockerell and preface by John Plummer [New York, 1969], pp. 64, 65), the gallows of the king of Ai has a cross-arm, but the whole is tilted diagonally on a pivoted contrivance, perhaps to distinguish it from the Cross. S. Cockerell, in editing this manuscript, misinterpreted the gallows as a military engine. The same instrument, tilted diagonally, is represented in the Bodleian Moralized Bible on f. 202, 204, in the scene of the hanging of Haman. The Vulgate text of Esther 5:14, illustrated there, also refers to the gallows as *crux* (*iussit excelsam parari crucem* [5:14]; *ipsum iussi affigi cruci* 18:7]). Haman on the gallows is likened to those who suffer torture in hell for having tortured others.

On the other side, the Jewish legend of Haman assimilated his cross to that of Christ (see L. Ginzberg, *The Legends of the Jews* VI p. 479, n. 184) and in response the Theodosian Codex (A.D. 408) prohibited the Jews from celebrating the Purim feast in which the crucifixion and burning of Haman in effigy were understood to be a mocking of Christ. Under Basil I (ca. 871–875) the formula of abjuration of Judaism by converts in Byzantium still refers to the mocking of Haman on a gibbet surmounted by a cross in the Purim celebration (see L. Bréhier, *La civilisation byzantine* [Paris, 1950], p. 303).

Edgar Wind ("The Crucifixion of Haman," *Journal of the Warburg and Courtauld Institutes* 1 [1937–38], 245–48) has argued ingeniously that Michelangelo, in representing Haman as crucified (on the Sistine ceiling), saw him as a tragic type and forerunner of Christ, in the sense of Frazer's thesis concerning the scapegoat or sacrificed redeemer. However, in Michelangelo's fresco Haman is nailed to a **Y**-shaped stake, with one leg free and bent and the whole body foreshortened, in a manner that suggests the thief who was crucified beside Christ in Renaissance compositions; and since, moreover, Haman on the ceiling is the counterpart at the left to the brazen serpent that symbolizes Christ at the right, one can interpret Michelangelo's thought in another sense: that the crucified Haman who wished to destroy the Jews is no innocent victim or redeemer but the evil opposite of the brazen serpent that heals and saves.

[64] See H. Omont, *Psautier de Saint Louis: Reproduction des 92 miniatures du ms. latin 10525* (Paris, n.d.), pl. XXIX, LX, LXXIX.

[65] On Joseph as a type of Christ, see M. Schapiro, "The Joseph Scenes on the Maximianus Throne," *Gazette des Beaux-Arts*, 6th series, 40 (1952), 27–38.

[66] See A. de Laborde, *La Bible Moralisée Illustrée* (Paris 1911–27), 5 vols.

[67] Honorius Augustodunensis, *Gemma Animae* I, cap. xliv, xlv, Pat. lat., CLXXII, cols. 557–58. For a similar comparison of Moses' raised hands with those of the priests and bishops in prayer, which assure victory to the faithful, see the *Commentary on Exodus* by Bruno of Asti (early 12th century), Pat. lat., CLXIV, cols. 271–72. Interesting for the shift to the ecclesiastical interpretation is that Bruno takes account here of Exodus 17:9 and says that Moses stands on the hilltop holding the rod in his hand as the bishops and those on the higher thrones of the church carry a staff in their hands for the correction and guidance of the faithful. The likeness of Moses to the priest at the Mass is affirmed by Peter Comestor in his retelling of the story in the *Historia Scholastica*, Exodus Ch. XXXV, Pat. lat., CXCVIII, col. 1161: "in huius rei figura sacerdos manus elevat in missa, etiam in figura Christi orantis in cruce." Pertinent to the liturgical symbolism is also the explanation in the *Glossa Ordinaria*, a compilation of the 12th century (Pat. lat., CXIV, cols. 242–43)—Moses' hands are raised not outstretched. To raise the hands is an act of raising oneself to God "…elevat manus, non extendit…Elevare

manus hoc est actus levare ad Deum…Elevat ergo manus qui thesaurizat in coelo"—an interpretation that recalls the rabbinical comments cited above in note 19. But the Gloss also compares the raised hands with the Passion of Christ and the defeat of the devil. For the acquaintance of Christian scholars of the 12th century with Jewish exegesis see Beryl Smalley, *The Study of the Bible in the Middle Ages* (University of Notre Dame Press, 1964), pp. 149 ff. and 161 ff. on Andrew of St. Victor. For the pictorial parallel there is a miniature in the Hortus Deliciarum of Herrade of Landsberg (1167–95), showing Moses at the battle, standing behind an altar, with arms held up by Aaron and Hur—see *Herrade de Landsberg, Hortus Deliciarum*, ed. by A. Straub and G. Keller (Strasbourg, 1901), pl. XIVbis (Supplément).

Another liturgical interpretation interesting for the new symbolism of the scene is that of the exegetist Hugo of St. Cher (+1263): "it is because the weary Moses prays sitting that the elders in the church of Paris sit during the Secret of the Mass and in this posture also symbolize the apostles sitting while Christ prays on the Cross; in many churches the old and young stand alike and express thereby Joshua and his army fighting against Amalek" (Hugonis de Sancto Charo, *Opera Omnia* [Venice, 1703], I, p. 86).

[68] For this Bible see Max Friedländer, *Die Lübecker Bibel* (Munich, 1923). Cf. also the Catalonian miniature of the 14th century in Paris (H. Omont, *Psautier illustré: Reproduction des 107 miniatures du manuscrit latin 8846 de la Bibliothèque Nationale* [Paris, n.d.], pl. 76, Psalm 114); the 15th-century Castilian Bible of the Duke of Alba (Roxburghe Club facsimile [Madrid, 1918–21], I, opp. p. 187).

An early example is a drawing in an immense picture Bible from Pamplona (Harburg ms. I,2, lat. 4°, 15, f. 59v), made for Sancho the Strong, king of Navarre (1194–1234). Aaron in near-profile stands at the left with a tau staff, like an abbot's, and Moses kneels at the right with hands raised in profile. An inscription reads: "Moyses orat." The battle lakes place below. See François Bucher, *The Pamplona Bibles* II (New Haven, 1970), pl. 122.

[69] Cf. the Bible of Sixtus IV (Venice, apud Juntas, 1616), p. 60; and a Bible of 1603 (Venice, Damianus Zenarius), p. 50.

[70] In a painting by Poussin in the Hermitage, Leningrad, Moses is shown in a near-frontal view with arms extended beside the kneeling Aaron and Hur; but it was not Poussin's intention to present the episode as a symbolic one through Moses' posture, for he has reduced Moses to a barely visible figure far off in the distance while the battle itself occupies the whole foreground and middle depth. The painting is rightly labeled: "The Victory of Joshua over the Amalekites." See A. Blunt, *Nicholas Poussin* II (New York, 1967), pl. 5.

[71] It is now in the Church of St. Remi in Reims.

[72] For the interest of Christian scholars in the Hebrew text of the Bible during the later Middle Ages, see B. Smalley, 1964: 338 ff. See also note 22 above on the rare occurrence of the singular *manum* in this context at an earlier date.

[73] See p. 61 of the facsimile (n. 63 above); the inscription reads: "Qualiter Amalech bellum infert filiis israel et Iosue iubente Moyse instructa acie occurrit hostibus." Nevertheless in the picture of Abraham's Sacrifice (p. 35), Isaac is shown with two crossed bundles of faggots, the angel crosses his arms in staying Abraham's sword and pointing to the ram, and the latter's horns are caught between two branches of a tree. Yet these details are so little stressed that one may explain them as devices of composition, utilizing older models, without a primary symbolical content.

[74] The same woodcut was used in the Lyons Bible of 1538, printed by Trechsel, and in other Bibles. The crossed hands still appear in the St. Louis Psalter, Bibl. nat. lat. 10525 (Omont, n.d.: pl. XXVII). In Queen Mary's Psalter in the British Museum, an English book of the early 14th century, the blessing itself is not shown but only the aftereffect on the feelings of Joseph and his sons. The French text says that Joseph was incensed because the blessing had been given to Ephraim whom he loved less. See Sir George Warner, *Queen Mary's Psalter* (London, 1912), pl. 37 and p. 66. (Perhaps after the expulsion of the Jews from England in 1290 the symbolism of the episode had lost its polemical interest.) Already in the 12th century Peter Comestor in retelling the story makes no reference to the Cross or the Messiah or Christ (*Historia Scholastica*, ch. 101). On the history of the illustration of this subject see W. Stechow, "Jacob Blessing the Sons of Joseph," *Gazette des Beaux-Arts* 23 (1943), 193–208.

[75] *De Legibus* 17 (I, 48–49). I cite this text after the valuable little work of Johan Chydenius, *The Theory of Medieval Symbolism* (= *Societas Scientiarum Fennicarum, Commentationes Humanarum Litterarum* XXVII:2) (Helsingfors, 1960), pp. 20–22.

[76] *The Uniqueness of the Individual* (New York, 1958), p. 74.

[77] As on the ivory cover of the Drogo Sacramentary (ca. 830), where all the figures in the nine scenes of ritual are in profile (A. Goldschmidt. *Die Elfenbeinskulpturen* I [Berlin, 1914], pl. XXX, no. 80b). Also in the miniature paintings in the same manuscript (W. Koehler, *Die Karolingischen Miniaturen* III [Berlin, 1960], pl. 83e, 84b). Carolingian art is in many respects a classic revival like the Latin poetry of the same time and conceives the ritual as an action of the priest or bishop much as the Roman artist, before the age of Constantine, represented ceremonies on the arches of triumph. For the later examples see the psalter, Paris, Bibliothèque de l'Arsenal ms. 1186 (H. Martin, *Psautier de Saint Louis et Blanche de Castille* [Paris, n.d.], pl. 43, for the near-profiles of the priests at the altar, and pl. 20, for the strict profiles of the Jews worshiping the golden calf, while a Christ in three-quarters view gives the tablet to a near-frontal Moses).

[78] A comparable conception of the ritual as exhibiting the hierarchical relations is the pair of ivory plaques of the 9th century in Frankfurt and Cambridge, England, with a beautiful gradation from frontal to profile, large to small, in two liturgical scenes (Goldschmidt, 1914: pl. LIII).

[79] Such an image of Christ in the church of Hagia Sophia is described by Jacopo Voragine in the chapter of the *Golden Legend* on the Feast of the Finding of the Cross (May 3). This appearance of the frontal head was noted also by Nikolaos Mesarites in his *ekphrasis* on the mosaics of the Church of the Holy Apostles in Constantinople (ca. 1200); he says of the Pantokrator image on the dome: "His look is gentle and wholly mild, turning neither to the left nor the right, but wholly directed toward all at once and at the same time toward each individually" (transl. by G. Downey, *Transactions of the American Philosophical Society*, N.S. 47 [1957], 870). In the preface of his *De Visione Dei*, Nicholas of Cusa cites as examples of an all-seeing image a bowman aiming an arrow in the marketplace of Nuremberg, Roger van der Weyden's work in the Town Hall in Brussels, a St. Veronica in Brixen, and for his teaching proposes an icon of God as all-seeing, the eyes seeming to move and follow the observer. There is also a Hebrew Midrashic text in which God is likened to a statue that looks at everyone (N. Glatzer, *Hammer on the Rock* [New York], p. 41). Pliny already notes this effect in his *Natural History* 35:37, in writing of the artist Famulus; he painted a Minerva "who faced the spectator at whatever angle she was looked at." The same effect was attributed in the 2nd century A.D. to an idol in Lucian's work *On the Syrian Goddess*, 32—"And there is still another astonishing thing about this idol: if one stands directly in front of it, she looks at you and follows you when you change your position. And if from another point a new spectator fixes his eyes on her, the goddess will also look at him." The phenomenon was described by Ptolemy in his *Optics*, a work that was available to the Latin West since the 12th century in a translation by the Sicilian admiral Eugenius: "It is thought that the image of a face painted on a tablet looks at the viewer though the image does not move, since a true glance is discerned only through the stability of the form of the same visual ray that falls on the depicted face....When therefore the viewer moves, the ray of vision moves and the viewer thinks the image is following him with its glance, while he is viewing it" (from the Latin translation by Ammiraglio Eugenio, ed. by G. Govi [Turin, 1885], p. 55).

[80] *Correspondances*. Cf. also the lines of Gérard de Nerval in *Vers Dorés*:

> Crains, dans le mur aveugle un regard qui t'épie
> . . . .
> Et comme un oeil naissant couvert par ses paupières,
> Un pur esprit s'accroit sous l'écorce des pierres!

The uncanny glance of the frontal eyes in a portrait head is a theme in Gogol's *The Portrait*, and Mathurin's *Melmoth the Wanderer*.

[81] Around 1200 the standard profile view of animals and especially of horses and lions is sometimes replaced by a foreshortened front view of the entire figure—an example of the growing interest in spatial depth and perspective. Earlier there existed the type of profile animal body with frontal head, and in medieval heraldry one came to distinguish the lion from the leopard by the latter's frontal head, both animals having profile bodies (see J. Klanfer, "Theorie des heraldischen Zeichen," p. 73, an unpublished doctoral thesis [Vienna University], for a copy of which I am indebted to the kindness of Dr. F. Novotny).

[82] In a marginal drôlerie in ms. 78 D 40, Royal Library, The Hague, a fox in Franciscan dress and a wolf in Dominican kneel in profile before a crowned frontal lion; Lillian M. C. Randall, *Images in the Margins of Gothic Manuscripts* (Berkeley, 1966), FIG. 497.

[83] For the different conceptions of this theme, see R. Hamann, "Die Salzwedeler Madonna," *Marburger Jahrbuch für Kunstwissenschaft* 3 (1927), 77–144, pl. XXVIII–LXIII, and especially pl. XLIII, XLIV.

[84] "Adversus Albigensium Errores," *Maxima Bibliotheca Veterum Patrum* XXV (Lyons, 1677), 222.

[85] Quintilian, *De Institutione Oratoria*, II, xiii, 12.

[86] Op. cit., p. 223 ff.—"ad derisum et opprobrium Christi."

[87] On the role of the glance, both profile and frontal, in the group portraits of the 16th and 17th centuries where it is a major factor in the structure and expression of the painting, see the still too little known work of Alois Riegl, *Das holländische Groppenporträt*, 2nd ed. (Vienna, 1931). I may note here that in the painting of the later 19th and early 20th centuries, the starkly frontal face and the pairing of frontal and profile returned as elements of the strong expressionist trend, both in portraits and narrative themes. The frontal position in subjects of sorrow, death, jealousy, anxiety, panic, and despair by Munch and Ensor is a means in portraying the person in distress, self-isolating and turned away from others—he cannot "face" the world; it is also a means of engaging the viewer's attention to the subject's face as that of another and kindred self-preoccupied with its own overpowering feelings and speaking out to the viewer. A different use of the contrast of frontal and profile, in a subtle novelistic spirit, is the painting by Vuillard, "The Artist's Mother and Sister" (ca. 1900, Museum of Modern Art, New York), where, in a marked perspective, the mother in black sits in front view before a massive reddish bureau in a plane parallel to the picture surface; the shy daughter, in a shrinking profile, stands at the side close to the mottled papered wall with which

she seems to merge through her patterned dress. A few years before, the Impressionist Renoir portrayed a daughter frontally and the mother at the side, without tension.

[88] On profile and full-face in Greek art, see M. Hoernes, *Urgeschichte der bildenden Kunst in Europa*, 3rd ed. (Vienna, 1925), pp. 592 ff., and H. Kenner. *Weinen und Lachen in der griechischen Kunst* (= *Österreiche Akademie der Wissenschaft, Philos.-hist. Kl.*, *Sitzungsberichte* 234, Bd.2 (Vienna, 1960), pp. 40 ff.

[89] For the contrast of the living figure and the image within a representation, there is an interesting example in a Greek vase painting with an actor in profile holding in his hands a frontal mask (K. Schefold, *Classical Greece* [London, 1967], color plate). Cf. also an Early Christian sarcophagus fragment in Florence with a relief of Nebuchadnezzar and the three Hebrew boys all in profile before the frontal sculptured head of an idol (*Zeitschrift für Kirchengeschichte* 54 (1935), 18 ff. and pl. I). In Titian's portrait of the so-called "Schiavone," there is a reverse choice: the living woman is frontal and the nearby relief is of a profile bust of a woman, perhaps a relative of the main subject. The choice here may depend on a convention for representing together a major and a minor figure in a double portrait, as in Domenico Ghirlandaio's of Francesco Sassetti and his little son in the Metropolitan Museum in New York.

[90] See E. Kühnel, *Miniaturmalerei im Islamischen Orient* (Berlin, 1923), pl. 3, 4, 5.

[91] Kühnel, 1923: Pl. 1, 7, and R. Ettinghausen, *Arab Painting* (1962), pp. 71, 85. There are examples with all figures in profile; Kühnel, pl. 10, 11. But as in Western medieval art the three-quarters head is the common form and the profile and front views are the marked variants. The profile sometimes appears in a corner or near the frame and helps to accent a direction of action.

[92] Cf. "The Sculptures of Souillac," cited above, note 9. For details see A. K. Porter, *Romanesque Sculpture* (1923), ill. 347, 348. In the Stuttgart Psalter, f. 126 (see the DeWald facsimile), Judas is frontal and is struck by the profiled Satan; in the Moralized Bible, Bodleian ms. 270b, f. 7v, Satan, pictured as an idol in a painting with shutters like an altarpiece, is in profile, and the figures worshiping him are in strict profile.

[93] Cf. the pictures in the manuscript of the *Cantigas de S. Maria* in the Escorial; J. Guerrero Lovillo, *Miniatura Gotica Castellana, siglos XlII y XIV* (Madrid, 1956), pl. 4, 5, 6, 8, 9.

[94] As in the Beatus Apocalypse of Saint-Sever, Paris Bibl. nat. ms. lat. 8878, f. 145v—W. Neuss, *Die Apokalypse des hl. Johannes in der altspanischen und altchristlichen Bibel-Illustration* (Münster i.W., 1931), FIG. 137.

[95] Omont, n.d. pl. IV, VIII, XI, LX, LXXXV. A particularly clear example of the use of frontal, three-quarters, and profile positions in a narrative picture as distinctions of spiritual and social rank is the fresco of St. Clement in the church of his name in

Rome. (See L. Coletti, *Die frühe Italienische Malerei* [Vienna 1949], pl. 9.) The bishop-saint with raised arms at the altar is strictly frontal, the congregation around him are in three-quarters or near-frontal view; the slave who leads away the blinded pagan antago-nist Sisinnius is in profile; below, the blind pagan, in near frontal posture, orders in abu-sive vernacular the arrest of Clement; instead, the slaves in profile bind and carry off a heavy column.

[96] This duality of the position or view should not be confused with the idea of Freud—a mistaken one, I believe (see E. Benveniste, "Remarques sur la fonction du langage dans la découverte freudienne," *Psychanalyse* 1 [1956]. 3–16, now reprinted in *Problèmes de la linguistique générale* [Paris, 1968], 75–87), that in primitive language the same word had contradictory meanings *(Gegensinn der Urworte)*, like certain symbols in dreams. In pictures the profile and frontal are positions with respect to a viewer, that distinguish and accent by contrast the already fixed meanings and qualities of rep-resented objects. Frontal and profile here are more like stress in speech or like the expressive use of the initial position for a word in a sentence, in departure from ordi-nary syntax.

[97] For an early example cf. the profile heads of Caiaphas and other Jews, in con-trast to the three-quarters head of Christ, in the *Hours of Salisbury*, ca. 1280; E. G. Millar, *English Illuminated Manuscripts from the Xth to the XIIIth century* (Brussels, 1926), pl. 97. Cf. also in a mid-14th-century manuscript of canon law, British Museum Royal 6 E VII, f. 341, the picture of Christians in three-quarters view arguing with heretics and Jews who have strictly profile heads with caricatured features—B. Blumenkranz, *Le juif médiéval au miroir de l'art chrétien* (Paris, 1966), FIG. 26, p. 33. In a Bible of the late 12th century—Paris, Bibl. nat. lat. 16746, f. 80v (possibly from Troyes)—Paul addressing the Jews sits in profile with legs crossed, but his head is a beautiful full face, while the Jews are sharply characterized in their profile heads.

[98] A. K. Porter, 1923: ill. 1320.

[99] Thus the expressiveness of Goya's portrait (in the Minneapolis Museum) of himself undergoing a heart attack is inconceivable in a profile or near-profile view.

[100] On this aspect of color see the important work of G. J. von Allesch, *Die aes-thetische Erscheinungsweise der Farben* (Berlin, 1925).

[101] *Roman Questions* XXVI, transl. by H. J. Rose (1924), p. 131.

[102] A parallel to this equipollence of black and white as symbolic colors is the use of both square and circle as models of divine being in religious imagination. Irenaeus says of certain Gnostics: "as by some similitude of a sphere or a square, they affirm the Father to comprehend within himself all ways, in the likeness of a sphere or in a quad-rangular form" (Irenaeus, *Five Books against Heresies*, transl. by J. Keble [1972], p. 125).

111

The varying symbolic sense of an object, rooted in its multiple qualities, was recognized by medieval writers who noted, e.g., that the lion could stand for both Satan and Christ. Cf. Peter of Poitiers: "As many significations of spiritual and invisible things can be discovered in corporeal and visible ones as these have properties, whether of inner nature or external form" (in rebus visibilibus...tot possunt reperiri spiritualium rerum et invisibilium significationes quot in ipsis visibilibus et corporalibus rebus inveniuntur proprietates, sive intus in natura, sive in forma foris)—see *Peter Pictavensis Allegoriae super Tabernaculum Moysi*, ed. by Ph. S. Moore and J. A. Corbett (Notre Dame, Indiana, 1938), cap. I, p. 3. Similarly, his contemporary, Alexander Neckam, observed that the symbolism of the serpent (= Satan, Christ, prudence, the year, etc.) varied "secundum diversarum naturarum schemata" of the creature (*De naturis rerum*, cap. CIX—de vulgari serpente—ed. Thomas Wright [London, 1863], p. 190).

PHOTO CREDITS

FIG. 1   After E. DeWald, *The Utrecht Psalter*, n.d., pl. XLb.

FIGS. 2, 3, 20 A. de Laborde, *La Bible Moralisée*, I, 1911, pls. 15, 16, 51.

FIG. 4   J. Wilpert, *Die römischen Mosaiken und Malereien der kirchlichen Bauten vom 4. bis 13. Jahrhundert*, Freiburg, 1916, pl. 20.

FIGS. 5, 6   A. Grabar, *The Beginnings of Christian Art, 200–395*, New York, 1967, FIGS. 97, 239.

FIG. 7   M. von Oppenheim, *Tell Halaf*, London and New York, n.d., pl. VIIIb.

FIG. 8   H. Omont, *Miniatures des plus anciens manuscrits grecs de la Bibliothèque Nationale*, Paris, 1929, pl. LV.

FIG. 9   W. Neuss, *Die katalanische Bibelillustration*, 1922, pl. 1.

FIG. 10   A. Goldschmidt, *German Book Illumination*, New York, 1928, pl. 72.

FIG. 11   P. E. Schramm and F. Mütherich, *Denkmale der deutschen Könige und Kaiser*, Munich, 1962, pl. 117.

FIG. 12   Photo, Bibliothèque Nationale, Paris.

FIG. 13   Photo, British Museum, London.

FIG. 14   *Encyclopedia Judaica*, Berlin, 1939, vol. 9, frontispiece.

FIG. 15   W. von Hartel and F. Wickhoff, *Die Wiener Genesis*, Vienna, 1895, pl. XLV.

FIG. 16   Count du Mesnil du Buisson, *Les Peintures de la Synagogue de Doura-Europos*, Rome, 1939, pl. XXIII.

FIGS. 17–19   H. Omont, *Psautier de Saint Louis, Reproduction des 92 miniatures du ms. latin 10525 de la Bibliothèque Nationale*, Paris, n.d., pls. XXXIV, XXXV, XVI.

FIG. 21   M. Friedländer, *Die Lübecker Bibel*, Munich, 1923, pl. 25.

FIG. 22   Kunsthistorisches Institut, Universität Marburg, courtesy of Professor

114

SCRIPT
IN
PICTURES:

Semiotics of Visual Language

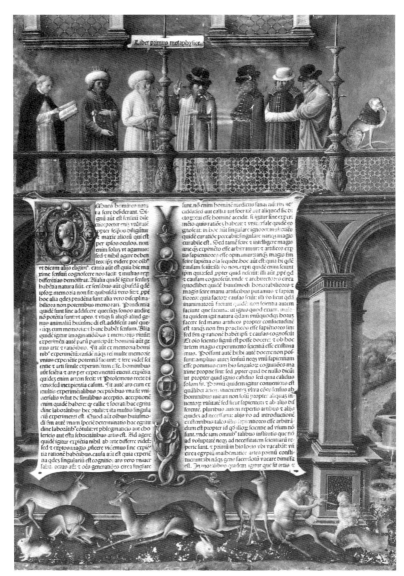

FIG. 1. New York, The Pierpont Morgan Library, *Aristotle's Works*, 3rd edition, Torresanus and Blavis, *The Seven Philosophers*, 1483.

SCRIPT IN PICTURES: SEMIOTICS OF VISUAL LANGUAGE

Medieval art is in two senses an art of the book. Its subject matter, in a great range of techniques, is founded on sacred texts that shaped religious life. The spiritual content of these writings entered into the allusive expressiveness of the work of art. In the second place, the sacred manuscript, with its paramount importance in cult and religious thought, became an object and field of art in itself, with qualities of its own and the source of an acknowledged merit for one who commissioned or transcribed or decorated the written text. In no other epoch has the book been for generations, even for centuries, as it was throughout the Middle Ages, a prime field of invention of styles of art and the expression of individual sensibility and perceptions. In this double sense one may speak of medieval art as a book art.

The nature of the book entails for the painter who illustrates it a special problem that is the subject of this study. As a written work the book is a field of non-mimetic visual signs—called conventional or arbitrary by students of the language—that elicit in the reader a prescribed mode of perception (in time). The reader scans the words from left to right or right to left, depending on the language, and follows a strict order of successive horizontal alignments from top to bottom of the leaf. A drawing or painting on the written field poses for the artist a problem: how to integrate the script on the surface of the page with the freer order of an image of state or action in a suggested spatial depth. The picture itself may include bits of writing; these are not only labels that help the reader to identify the subject; they sometimes depict speech naively as a string of letters issuing from the mouth of a person represented *in* the miniature—speech as an act is simulated through words in the picture. Speech belongs to the speaker in a way different from the words on the adjoining text. In some medieval book illustrations and also in sculptures, mosaics, and wall paintings, the figures hold scrolls on which their recorded speech is transcribed. The scroll itself becomes a sign of speech. There are many examples of scenes in which a dialogue is accompanied by a virtual combat of scrolls as signs of contending speech, though nothing is written on them.

When introduced into a picture, the written word may lead to anomalies of space composition, a challenge to the modern reader's perception of the painting as a consistently ordered artistic whole. This device may seem less strange to one who is accustomed to medieval books in which words appear in the pictures as well as nearby on the written page, or to one who knows the comic strips of our own century and takes it for granted that words can be enclosed in pictures, as in the balloons issuing from the mouths of the figures. In the past these were sometimes regarded as naive or vulgar, a lower though attractive art. For the Classic taste of the fourth century B.C. and for the Renaissance, and in certain phases of late medieval art, that insertion of the written word in the pictured action or landscape was felt to be bizarre. Aristotle, commenting on defective definitions of a concept or an object—those in which one cannot tell what is being defined—likened them to the works of the old painters whose subjects would be unintelligible if they were not explained by inscriptions in the space of the picture. The same idea was expressed by Giorgio Vasari in speaking of the use of inscribed rolls in pictures of an action; they are, he said, a crutch for one who has not yet learned to walk alone on his two feet. In the later Renaissance, the conception of the painting as a unified whole, given to the eye as a coherent visual object—what the English philosopher the earl of Shaftesbury called "eusynoptic"—excluded writing from a picture, since script, as a sequence of arbitrary marks, does not belong to the same order of signs as the pictorial ones that image recognizable bodies, faces, gestures, costumes, in a corresponding intelligible form.

Another difficulty with the insertion of script in a picture is that the written word does not have for the eye the same relation to space as pictorial signs. The artist's signature in a painted landscape or interior is ordinarily set in the foreground of a simulated depth, like the trees and buildings and figures. Where is it virtually? Does it float or does it lie between a particular part of the landscape and the picture surface? Seen in depth it should receive light, cast a shadow, and submit to the gradations of distinctness owing to the mass of air between the foreground and the distance.

It should take its place in the space of the picture like the other elements of the scene that are distinguished in their relationship of planes and positions in an ordered sequence—as an object that lies between two other objects in depth in an unmistakable manner. That one attributed to the inscribed word in the old pictures an independent material existence and weight is intimated in folklore and commentary. A Jewish tale recounts that, when Moses, angered by his people's idolatry, was about to smash the Tablets of the Law, "he saw the writing vanish from them, and at the same time he became aware of their enormous weight; for while the celestial writing was upon them they carried their own weight and did not burden Moses, but with the disappearance of the writing all this changed." In another context in the Middle Ages, the words of prayer skipped by a distracted or inattentive Christian, like the errors and omissions of a scribe in copying a sacred book, were preserved in a sack and were to burden him in hell or purgatory after they had been weighed in the balance of sins and good deeds.

Various devices in that art bring out the material reality of the spoken and written word. Among them is the carving of stone inscriptions and the hammering of metal repoussé as salient forms of relief. The initial letters in manuscripts and even whole phrases at the beginning of a text were often shaped as living creatures or solid geometric forms modeled by light and shade. Even the written word or printed leaf could be represented as a monumental object in its own right suspended in three-dimensional space. A magnificent example is the opening text of a printed volume of Aristotle's works published in Venice in 1483 (FIG. 1). That page of print appears on an enormous simulated sheet of parchment virtually twelve or more feet long, hanging in front of a building from a balcony on which stand and converse the pagan and Christian scholars to whom Aristotle's words are addressed.

The need to make script part of an object in three-dimensional space, and to give it as tangible a presence and support of the same order of materiality as the adjacent human figures, buildings, and landscape, is evident in the attachment of signatures and other writing to objects in depth.

Consider, as an example, the signature in a view of the sea painted by Gustave Courbet (FIG. 2). His name stands up on the beach in the foreground, overlapping the sand and water behind it. What is that row of little black marks in the lower left in the seascape? What kind of objects do they represent? In recognizing them as the artist's signature, you know they do not signify in the same way as the painted marks around them, which call to mind so vividly the ocean and beach. The written name "Gustave Courbet" invites a mode of perception and interpretation different from that of the pictured scene. You locate the letters on the surface of the canvas rather than in the projected three-dimensional space of nature. Is it a defect in the painting, inconsistent with the spatial order of the depicted scene? It would have disturbed the purist taste of Shaftesbury, his ideal of the "eusynoptic" in painting and his distinction of the different types of "characters" or visual signs. Yet in shifting our attention from the picture as an image of a deep space to the painting as a pattern of varied tonal flecks on the flat surface plane of the canvas, we see the artist's name as a horizontal series of dark touches related to the dark of the distant boat on the horizon at the right; those touches on a light ground are an anchored set that, in our view of the painting as a whole, we couple on a

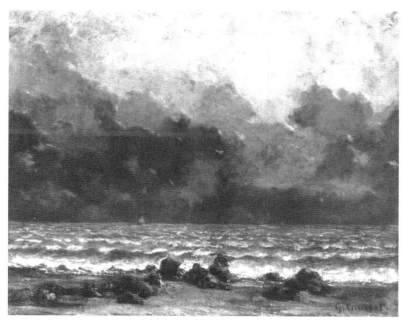

FIG. 2. New York, The Metropolitan Museum of Art, Gustave Courbet, *The Sea*

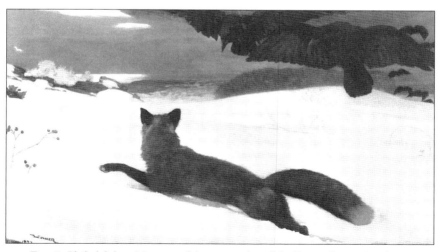

FIG. 3. Philadelphia, Museum of American Art of the Pennsylvania Academy
of the Fine Arts, Winslow Homer, *Fox Hunt*, 1893.

diagonal axis with the boat on a darker ground; the difference of relative value contributes to and reinforces our perception of the distance between foreground and horizon. Nevertheless, we sense a discrepancy of script and image, a difference between reading and viewing, no matter how the two types of signs are integrated and harmonized. We are induced to accept the signature in the ocean or on the beach as a convention, though it violates the consistency of the picture as a rendering of an actual site in nature.

In resolving the anomaly of a signature in the depth of a land-scape, the American painter Winslow Homer resorted to the device of inserting his name inside a deep, diagonal furrow in the snow pictured in the midspace of his *Fox-Hunt* (FIG. 3). He allowed the snow to mask the lower part of the letters of his name, as if to conceal, yet discreetly assert, the artist's presence inside the scene. Here, as in Courbet's picture, the name was designed to accord with an element of representation. In that signature, which is set so precisely within the depth of the pic-tured space and is overlapped by the furrow, the long tail of the *R* resembles the bushy tail of the fox above.

The same problem was resolved in a similar way by Édouard Manet in painting *The Fifer* (FIG. 4). He signed his name diago-nally so that the difference between ground plane and background is barely evident. Apparently, he wished to locate the signature in perspective space on the floor itself and to detach it from the lower, horizontal line. Through this inclined axis, it also rein-forces the shoe, its cast shadow, and the dark stripe on the trouser.

In another work, his *Portrait of Zola* (FIG. 5), Manet adopted the device known since the Renaissance, and perhaps earlier, of placing the artist's name on the surface of a distinct object inside

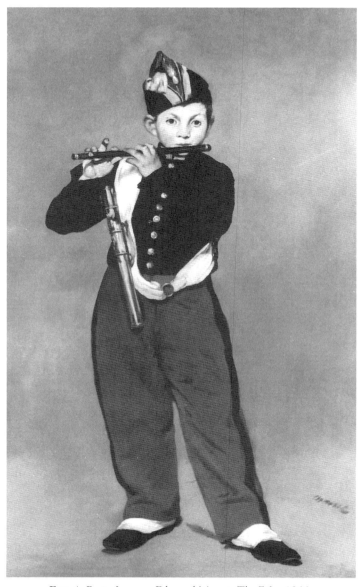

FIG. 4. Paris, Louvre, Edouard Manet, *The Fifer*, 1866.

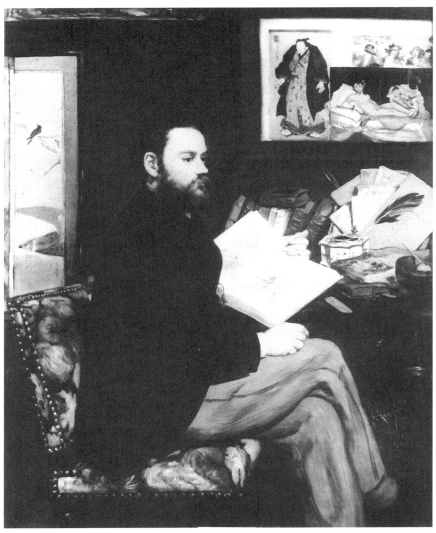

FIG. 5. Paris, Jeu de Paume, Edouard Manet, *Portrait of Emile Zola*, 1868.

the scene. Among the books on Zola's table is the one that he wrote in Manet's defense; on its cover is the painter's name, partly masked by the feather of a quill pen. As an element of the printed title, the name here has a local habitation and can take its unambiguous place in the ordered sequence of layered planes, depths, and varied surfaces represented in the picture space; its perspective determines the axis and angle of the book. This is a common solution to the problem of integrating the word, usually a single word, with the representation in which it has been placed.

In the Early Christian period the artist often had the task of portraying the four evangelists in gospel books and on the walls of churches. To distinguish them, he coupled each with a different symbol: John's was an eagle and Matthew's a man. But he could also identify each through an inscription on the book; the author's name or the first words of his Gospel were exposed on its open leaves. In the mosaic image of Saint Mark in San Vitale at Ravenna, you read in his book the words SECUNDUM MARCUM— the Gospel according to Saint Mark (FIG. 6). The letters are so big that they fill the two pages that are displayed *en face* to the viewer. But in Matthew's book (FIG. 7) the writing is illegible, though only slightly smaller than in Mark's. The leaves are turned, however, to the author-scribe, who is shown with pen in hand. The large wordlike marks are vertical, horizontal, and diagonal lines in regular alignment, perhaps intended to suggest the appearance of a capital script in a book seen at a distance. They may be explained also as an effort to simulate Hebrew writing— Matthew's Gospel was believed to have been composed originally in that language. On a nearby wall the prophet Jeremiah holds an extended scroll with illegible marks. But in the image of John,

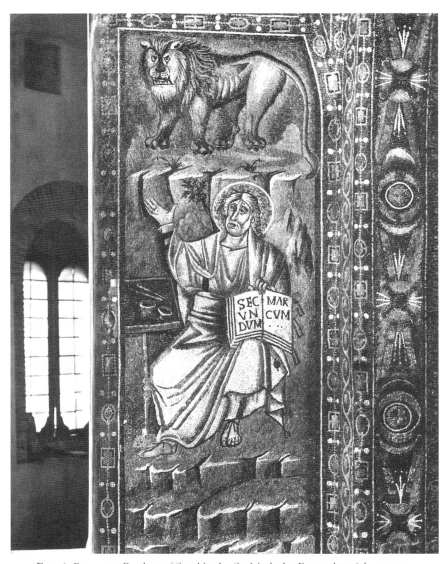

FIG. 6. Ravenna, Basilica of San Vitale, St. Mark the Evangelist, 6th century.

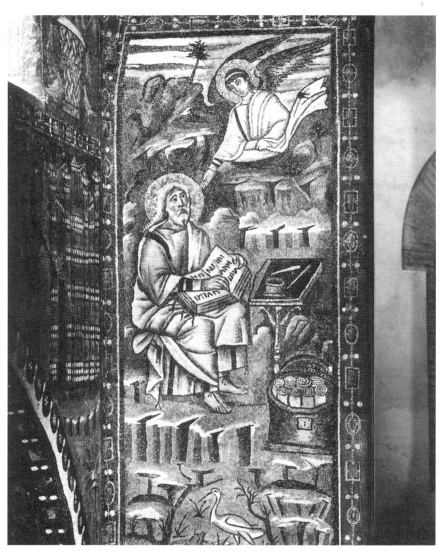

FIG. 7. Ravenna, Basilica of San Vitale, St. Matthew the Evangelist, 6th century.

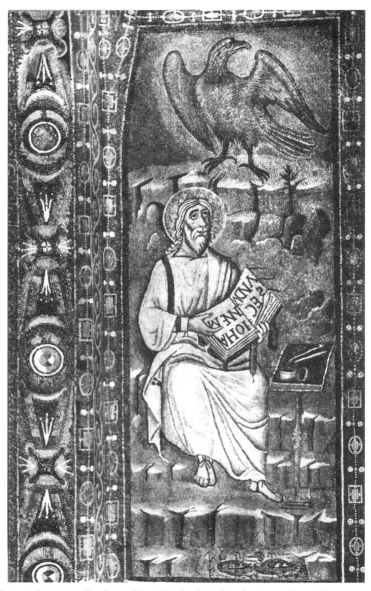

FIG. 8. Ravenna, Basilica of San Vitale, St. John the Evangelist, 6th century.

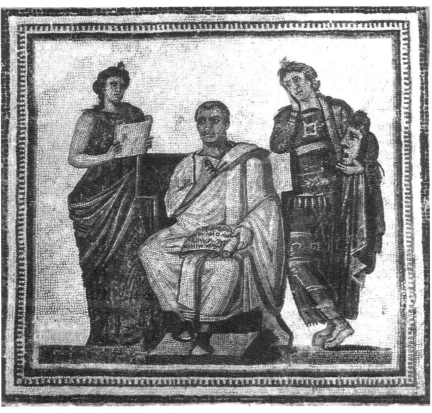

FIG. 9. Tunis, The Bardo National Museum, floor mosaic from Sousse, House of Virgil, Virgil lectures between two muses, 3rd century.

with the eagle above him, the two words *secundum Iohannem* are inscribed in big letters that fill the exposed pages of a book large enough to cover his lap (FIG. 8). From the spectator's viewing point the words look upside down, yet they are true to the pictured situation, since they face John, who reads in his own book.

These three mosaics show the different ways of inserting in a picture some written words addressed to the viewer. Mark and Luke hold up their open books for an external reader's literate eyes. John's writing is inverted to accord with the viewpoint of the evangelist himself as an internal viewer; whereas Matthew's is a set of illegible marks that render the appearance of writing to one who sees but cannot read because of his distance from the words either in space or in culture. All these are basic solutions found elsewhere in Early Christian art.

The inverted writing, which seems unclassical in its concession to the viewpoint of an internal reader, was known already in pagan art. In the famous mosaic of Virgil seated between two muses (FIG. 9), the poet holds a scroll with a passage from the *Aeneid* inscribed upside down from the spectator's point of view. It was not meant to be read by an external viewer; at least he cannot make out the words in the same glance by which he grasps the mosaic as a whole and recognizes the features in it. To read those words, he must accomplish in normal perception the feat of reading upside down, unless, of course, he moves around the pavement mosaic and inverts the figure of Virgil. The reading of inverted letters implies a rotation of the viewer's head or of the book on one plane; but this inscribed roll is not in a plane parallel to the picture surface. It is tilted in depth and corresponds to the foreshortened horizontal plane of Virgil's lap.

One might suppose that in classic art the inversion of script is an example of a "naturalistic" or "objective" attitude characteristic of that art; the script, as an attribute of the poet, is adjusted to his point of view in writing or reading. It is like the reflection of Narcissus in the Roman painting of that subject in Pompeii. The face in the water, relative to the viewer of the picture, is inverted, but adapted to the self-contemplating eye of Narcissus above. But there are enough instances in Greek and Roman pictorial art of the scroll and its writing turned to the spectator; in such a view of the writing the artist preserved its distinctness and completeness in what may be called an archaic object-oriented attitude.

The two opposed ways of representing an author together with his text reappear in a Greek Gospel manuscript of the tenth century from Mount Athos (FIG. 10). Saint Luke has before him a model from which he copies the text. This model is a roll; the transcript, a codex. In the first, the writing is a series of illegible cursive marks. They may be stenographic, but I incline to doubt it. They move on the surface of the roll, around and up and over, in three dimensions. The lines of writing are straight where the edges of the roll are straight; they curve as the roll unfurls. But the copied text in the writer's lap is composed of large uncials turned toward the author-scribe and are much too large for the page from a strict geometric-perspective point of view; four or five lines of writing fill a page. At that same distance we are unable to make out what is inscribed on the rolls nearby. In the different treatment of the script in the two texts, the artist seems to illustrate the content of the words on the open pages of Luke's codex. They are the first sentence of his Gospel and refer to the "many writers who have undertaken to draw up an account of the events that

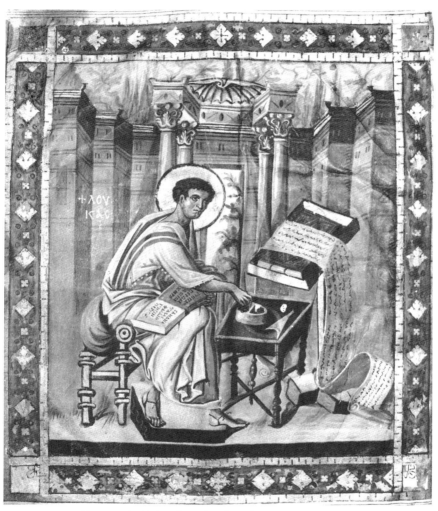

Fɪɢ. 10. St. Luke, Gospels, Mt. Athos, Stauronikita 43.

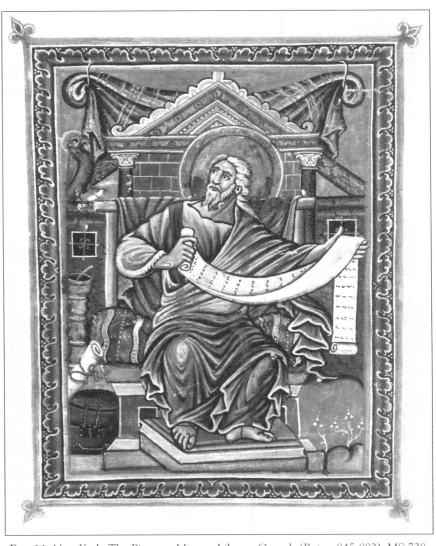

Fig. 11. New York, The Pierpont Morgan Library, Gospels (Reims 845-882), MS 728, St. John, fol. 141v.

have happened among us [Christians], following the traditions handed down by the original eyewitnesses and servants of the Gospel. And so I, in my turn, your Excellency, as one who has gone over the whole course of these events in detail, have decided to write for you a connected narrative." The scrolls hanging over the lectern may represent those older writings that Luke has consulted. The more distant and less ordered aspect of the writing on the scrolls corresponds, then, to the distance in time between those accounts and Luke's, the codex being the more recent form of the book. But the illegible forms of the writing may be, like the script in the Ravenna mosaics of Matthew and of Jeremiah, an attempt to simulate the exotic Hebrew script.

All three kinds of script in a picture survive together in the Western Middle Ages, though a school of painting will employ one variant more often than the others. It may be said that, from the eighth century to the fourteenth, all of them can be found somewhere in Europe and sometimes in works of the same school.

In a manuscript in the Morgan Library (Fig. 11), the evangelist holds a roll with little marks perpendicular to the long edge rather than the short; they are not meant to be read but simply to be viewed as the picture is viewed, as spots that appear on the vehicle, whether parchment or papyrus, like the tiny marks on a pictured distant building, which we recognize as windows; from such flecks we cannot make out the detailed structure of the windows in an Impressionist painting, but from their place in the context we know what they represent.

In a Gospel manuscript in the Stockholm Library, about which we have learned much from Carl Nordenfalk, the evangelist Matthew holds a roll suspended in his left hand, with the evange-

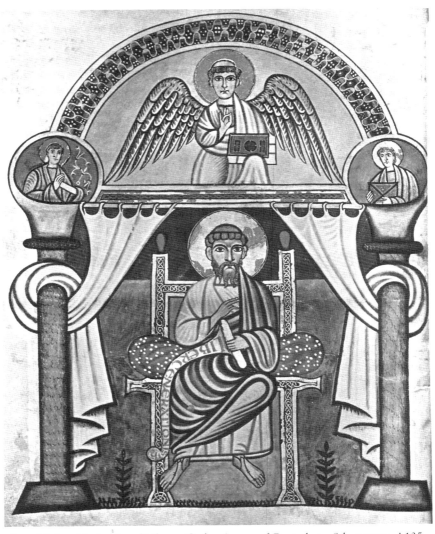

FIG. 12. Stockholm, Royal Library, Codex Aureus of Canterbury, 8th century, A135, St. Matthew, f.9v.

list's words inscribed distinctly, but inverted; they read downward from left to right, following the curve of the roll. The writing is adapted to Matthew's viewpoint, not the observer's (FIG. 12).

In contrast to this type is the medieval practice of displaying the two leaves of the book open as a single panel, a rectangle facing the viewer; across it the evangelist Matthew writes out the first words of his Gospel: *liber generationis Jesu Christi*, etc., in big letters for you to read like a framed sign (FIG. 13). Here the observer's point of view as a reader, and not Matthew's as a scribe, determines the axes of the writing. How are figure and script unified as a visual pattern? It is not easy to say; different adjustments of the eye come into play when we sight a human figure and read a text in the same field. One will, of course, see that the little black lines of those letters resemble other small units in the representation of the figure and its surrounding objects; the scale of writing is like that of the ornament and drapery folds and even of the facial features drawn on the same leaf. Are we perhaps rationalizing the coherence of picture and script? The common scale may result from an effort of unification; but what of the actual grid, the network of elements? The letters form a regular matrix that belongs to script, a pattern we do not find in the other parts, though the frame is rectangular and the rod and furniture sustain that form. At any rate, it is a problem for the observer, not for the artist who takes it in stride. He has found a method, a style, in which script and image can be joined so as to fit each other; their relation to the external reader is as important to the artist as the relation to the internal one—perhaps more important since what is pictured and written is a message, the sacred vehicle of life-giving religious ideas. But we

137

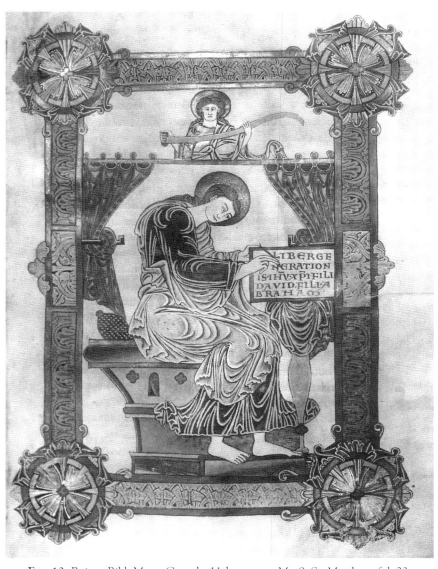

Fig. 13. Reims, Bibl. Mun., Gospels, 11th century, Ms. 9, St. Matthew, fol. 23.

may suppose, too, that a demand for clarity in this archaic art, as in children's drawings, entails the separation of the script as a part distinct from the rest and valued for itself; we can distinguish it and read it in isolation from everything around it.

Another characteristic feature in medieval art: not only is the script in this picture set like the ordinary matrix of writing on the page of text, but despite the scribe's hand covering part of the book represented in the picture, no word is incomplete. Hand and pen do not cover a single letter. The writing is isolated as a complete closed object regardless of what is in front of (or above) it, contrary to the parts of other elements of the drawing, which are cropped or overlapped.

Sometimes the need to accommodate the written word to an overlapping hand leads the artist to insert the hand within a word by separating disproportionately two of its letters and thereby breaking the expected uniform spacing of the word. In a scene of the Annunciation from the Glazier Hachette Psalter in the Morgan Library (FIG. 14), such a seeming violation can be explained by a symbolism in the resulting form. Here, the large interval between the A and the VE of AVE, formed by the angel's hand in a picture of his message to Mary, recalls the frequent medieval reading of AVE as A-VAE, i.e., "away with woe." It occurs often in hymns and other texts:

Sumens illud ave	*(Accepting that ave*
Nos emundans a vae	*Cleansing us of woe)*
Nostrum vae per ave tollis	*(Our woe through ave you remove*
Nomen Evae dum revolvis	*When you reverse the name of Eve.)*

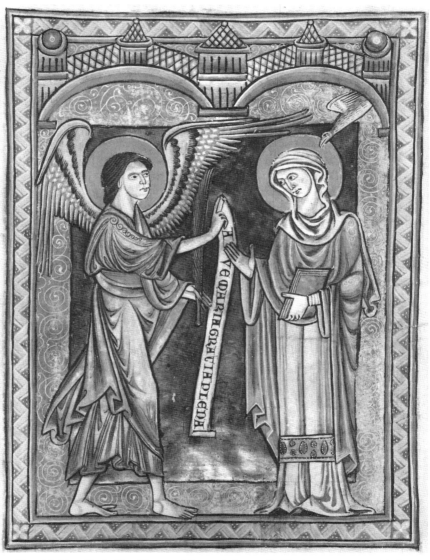

FIG. 14. New York, The Pierpont Morgan Library, G. 25, Annunciation, fol. 1v.

Overlapping is also an important space-shaping phenomenon; if B is overlapped by A, B will appear behind A. And if B overlaps C, then B will be seen between A and C. With a large enough series of such overlappings, considerable depth is suggested even where there is no convergence of perspective lines or foreshortening. (We must keep this in mind in judging the effects of spatial depth in medieval painting.)

The integrity of the writing in a picture is preserved already in Greek art of the sixth and fifth centuries B.C. In a vase painting, a teacher holds up an inscribed poetic text and recites or chants it before a pupil who is learning the poem; yet the writing is exposed in such a way that seemingly only the external viewer can read it (FIG. 15). The teacher's eyes are not directed toward it nor are the child's. From this pagan example we learn that the primitive form is neither uniquely Christian nor medieval; like the eye drawn *en face* in a profile head, it belongs to a certain stage in the development of pictorial art. That archaic style, in which the elements are distinct and as complete as possible, is followed by one with increased overlapping and continuity. Stated differently: the development is from a stage wherein each object is presented as if beheld from a point of view that preserves its fullness and distinctness, to one in which the position of an artist-spectator, unique and fixed, determines the apparent relationships of all objects to each other and to his point of sight, and entails in his picturing of that field the foreshortenings and overlappings that transform the constant shapes of objects, adapted to the ordered pattern of the whole.

We do not have to solve here the problem of the historical continuity of the Greek and medieval examples, but I may note that this archaic form is found in more than one cultural epoch.

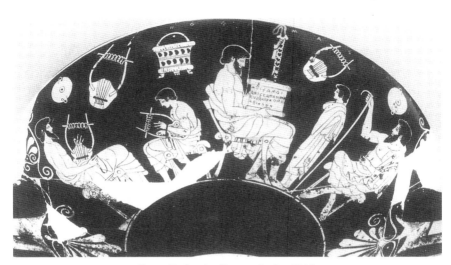

FIG. 15. Cup by Douris, Berlin 2285.

Classical tradition need not be the source of the medieval conception. It is highly improbable that an Anglo-Saxon artist in the eleventh century owed it to a Greek vase painting of the sixth or fifth century B.C., although features of a later, more naturalistic classic style were maintained in that medieval art.

In the ninth century A.D., artists who render the partly open erect book in a foreshortened perspective preserve the regular orthogonal matrix of writing. In a portrait of Matthew in a Gospel manuscript in Kremsmünster, the perspective view determines a zigzag outline of the book (FIG. 16). Simplified in form, the open leaves are symmetrical, but the lines of writing do not follow the convergence and foreshortening of the edges of the page. The word, as I have said, is indestructible and invariant, as on the Tables of Moses; it preserves its form and size, despite the perspective transformation of the boundary of the surface that carries the script. Submitted to a norm of legibility, the writing retains its orthogonal matrix no matter what the position of the painter-observer.

Another drawing in the same codex, the portrait of Mark, shows how that independent structure of the script, with its horizontal and vertical axes, is maintained in a picture (FIG. 17). Where the fully open book is laid out horizontally, as in the portrait of Mark, the matrix naturally coheres with the book's form.

The model of the book as a foreshortened zigzag pattern existed already in the fifth century A.D. It is found in the stucco figures of the Orthodox Baptistry in Ravenna (FIG. 18). While provincial in aspect, they betray in many details the copying of an older, more naturalistic classical work. We may call theirs a naive reductive style.

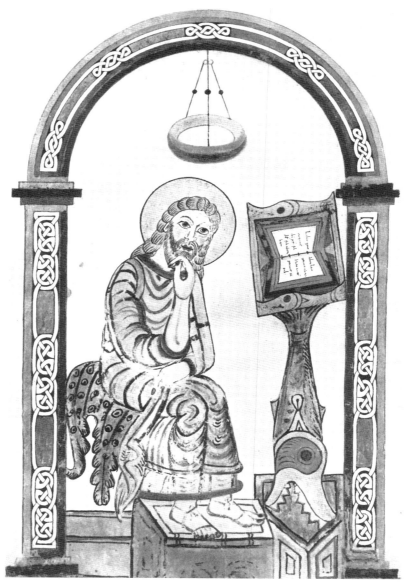

FIG. 16. Kremunster, Stiftsbibliothek, Codex Millenarius, Cim. 1, St. Matthew, f. 17v.

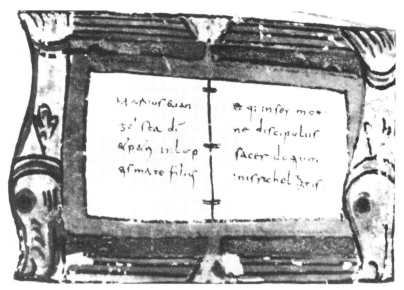

FIG. 17. Kremunster, Stiftsbibliothek, Codex Millenarius, Cim. 1, St. Mark (detail), f. 18.

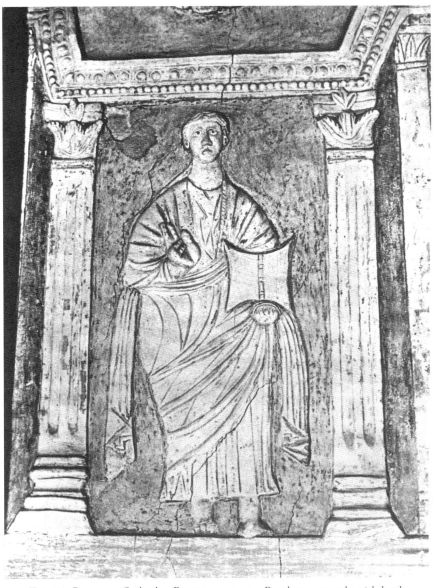

Fig. 18. Ravenna, Orthodox Baptistery, stucco, Prophet or apostle with book.

In a miniature in the Stuttgart Psalter, a manuscript of the early ninth century, the book itself is drawn in an angular view that suggests acquaintance with perspective forms; the sides are shown, as well as the front elevation; but the open book, perched on the front edge of the altar, stands up in an improbable way (FIG. 19). Yet it is a carefully considered drawing; we see how well the lines of the book have been fitted to the altar cloth and to the reversed convergence of the top edge of the altar.

Even where these are drawn more naturalistically, as in a miniature in Brussels where the left page of the open book is parallel to the picture plane and the much smaller right page is sharply foreshortened (FIG. 20), the inscription, *omnis scriptura divinitus inspirata*—"all scripture is divinely inspired"—is written across the two pages as if on one leaf; the words on the foreshortened *recto* are set on the same horizontal axis as those on the left. It is a clear illustration of that phenomenon of conservation of the script matrix in the picture plane even when attached to an object foreshortened in the third dimension.

Artists of the Middle Ages could, however, adapt the form of the script to make it adhere to the modeled three-dimensional form of an object. A beautiful example is a miniature in a Carolingian manuscript in the British Museum, Harley 647, the Latin translation of a poem by the Greek astronomer Aratus of Soli (FIG. 21). The figure of the zodiacal centaur is represented partly by a painting of the extremities and partly by inscribed verses that speak of the sign on the centaur's haunch. The words form wavy tracks, and through that curvature they model the form, giving it the fullness and convexity of the flank and rear of a horse.

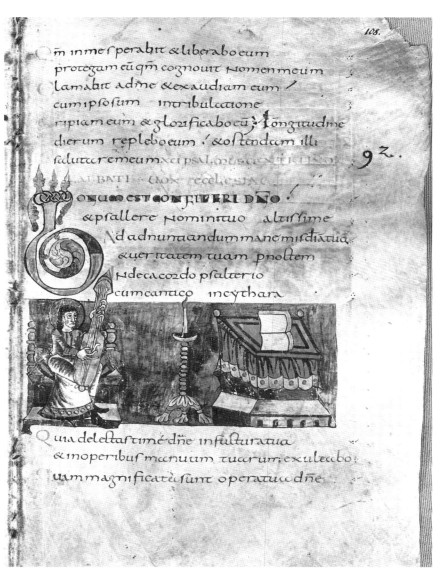

F<small>IG</small>. 19. Stuttgart, Württembergesche Landesbibliothek, Stuttgart Psalter, f. 108r.

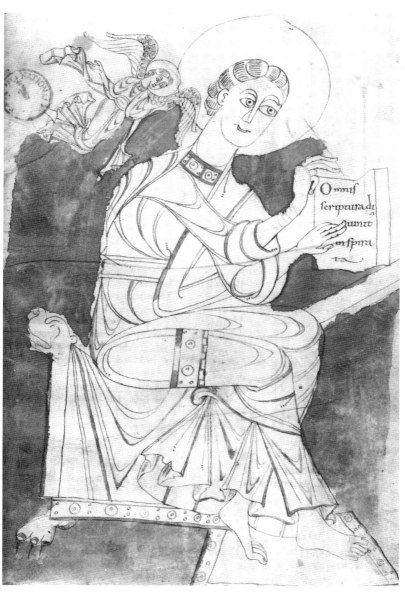

FIG. 20. Brussels, Bibliothèque Royale, MS 9071, St. Augustine, f. 2r.

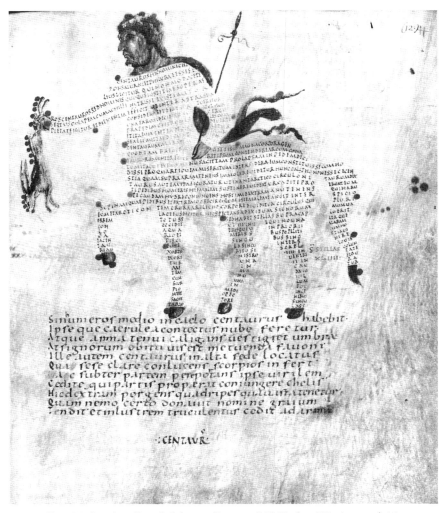

FIG. 21. London, British Library, Centaur, MS Harley 647, Aratus, f. 12.

150

Besides the external reader to whom the artist may address the inscription, in disregard of the viewpoint of the figure who writes or reads inside the picture, there is also an inner reader whose point of view the artist respects, even at the expense of the inscription's legibility to an external reader. A fine example is from a thirteenth-century German manuscript, the Goslar Evangeliary (FIG. 22). In a miniature at the beginning of Jerome's preface, addressed to Pope Damasus, who had asked him to translate the Bible, Jerome presents him his book with the open pages inscribed: "You pressed me to produce a new work from an old one, in making this new translation." The words, *novum opus me facere cogis ex vetere*, etc., are written upside down for the pope to read right side up. The pope, sitting above Jerome, is obviously not looking at the text from the same point of view as we are in reading the manuscript; we cannot make out the words unless we invert our eyes or the image. That inversion would be a rotation of the visible object; it is an early achievement of the child in judging the positions and forms of things. Here it is applied in a manner that seems to break with the logic of the virtual structure of the picture as a whole. Yet we are not disturbed; we are even charmed by the painter's naiveté and resoluteness in holding literally to the significance of a represented reader's internal viewpoint and sacrificing legibility from the viewpoint of the external observer.

Inversion of script need not always imply a reader from above. On a drawing of the bishop-saint Cunibert of Cologne addressing the kneeling chaplain of a confraternity, the words of the holy patron, in rhyming verses, are written upside down and form an arch above the head of the kneeling figure at the left. Had the

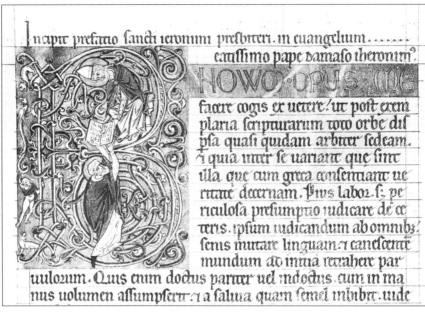

FIG. 22. Goslar, Rathaus, Gospel MS, Initial B, "Presentation of the Manuscript."

artist-scribe written them right side up, they would be reversed if the intention was to present them as issuing from Cunibert. In that inversion the left-to-right direction of both words and letters is preserved. The scribe has evidently turned the leaf 180° and written the inscription from left to right. For a speaking figure at the right, the emission of his words leftward would violate the usual order of written words. It is interesting that the scribe in the Cologne document of 1247 (now in the Staatsarchiv of Cologne cathedral in Düsseldorf), aware of the problem, has drawn at the first word of the inscription a short curved line as an indication of a scroll that the bishop-saint holds in his right hand; the inscription appears, then, as both speech and a written message.

By the fourteenth century, with the development of modeled sculpturesque forms in painting, artists began to adapt the inscribed words to the foreshortenings of a represented book or scroll. An interesting variant appears in an Italian miniature painting of about 1320 in the Morgan Library (FIG. 23). King David holds an open, suspended scroll on which the first syllables of *misere[b]it* are parallel to the short edge; the second, on a diagonal axis, follows the curve of the roll; the next one is cut off; pseudo-Oriental writing is embroidered on the horizontal hem of David's robe and on his sleeve. Different types of script are attached to material objects of three-dimensional form, with marked modeling and a play of the concave and the convex. Note the cropping of letters at the edge of the roll. It is an attempt to introduce overlapping and movement and to give solidity and depth to the objects to which the writing adheres. But the script itself lies on a single surface and relates to its background in quite other ways than the roll. In the course of the fourteenth and fif-

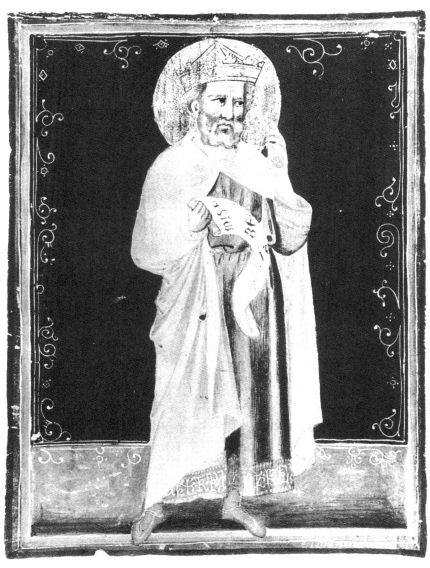

FIG. 23. New York, The Pierpont Morgan Library, MS 643,
Scenes from the Bible, King David, p. 1.

154

teenth centuries, with the development of a consistent perspective in painting, the script is submitted to the same projective rules as the book and other objects around it and subjected to the perspective of the whole.

As she writes, the Virgin Mary in Botticelli's *Madonna of the Magnificat* covers a large part of the writing with her hand; like her, the Child and the angel, touching the book, obscure the text. The reader can hardly make out the words; instead, he has a more vivid sense of the moment, the ongoing activity of writing, and of the book as an object of weight and volume; the open, inscribed page is a flexible surface in depth distinct from the others around it, yet coordinated with them in the perspective system. Since then, script within pictures has been attached to an object or a region of space that is submitted to the perspective viewpoint governing the picture as a whole. The written word in a picture is often foreshortened, with a progressive diminution of the letters in depth and with a convergence of the horizontal lines of its matrix, like the columns and trees in the same picture.

I turn to another aspect of script in a pictorial setting: the roll as a carrier and sign of speech. It is a feature we have seen in the portrayals of sacred figures but also, at times, in the picturing of their action or communication. In the portrait of Saint Luke in the Egbert Psalter (FIG. 24), the roll on his lap is bent in two places: parts overlap each other. Another kind of overlapping appears in a roll hanging over the lectern, and a third in the sym-

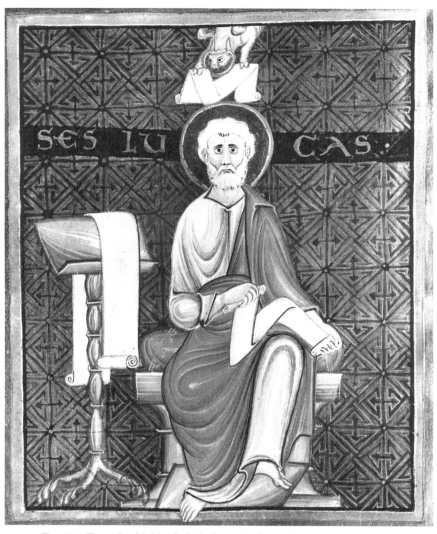

FIG. 24. Trier, Stadtbibliothek Cod. 24, Codex Egberti, Portrait of Luke.

156

bol of the evangelist above. The roll was identified with heaven and also with antiquity; sometimes it symbolized prophecy or the Old Testament. What concerns us here is not the specific symbolism but the representation of a roll without writing. As in the figure of speech called synecdoche—a part of an object standing for a whole, as "sail" for a "ship"—compare a "page" of Shakespeare for a writing. This tense, inspired figure of the evangelist-author forms, together with the horizontal inscription of his name, a cross that is traced countless times in the labyrinth of meanders in the background. The repeated roll, uninscribed, is a pronounced motif, an insistent attribute of Saint Luke as a man of the sacred Word, the evangelist who receives and copies a message from above.

The association of the roll with the individual—now preserved in our use of *role* to designate the behavior and function of a unique personality, with a prescribed message or theatrical performance of the word—is familiar to students of medieval art. It appears in the sixth century in paintings in the Rossano Gospels, a manuscript from Constantinople or other great center in the Near East (FIG. 25). A scene from the Gospel, the Parable of the Good Samaritan, is represented above four figures from the Old Testament who carry rolls inscribed with their sayings that commend a virtue or prophesy an action exemplified in the episode above them. That concept of prophecy was later dramatized in the annual Christmas play in which the old Jewish prophets came forth, each predicting in his own different words the coming of Christ as the Messiah. Recognized then as the older form of the book, the roll had both a historical sense and the value of a vehicle of ancient prophecy, an unfurling of the future.

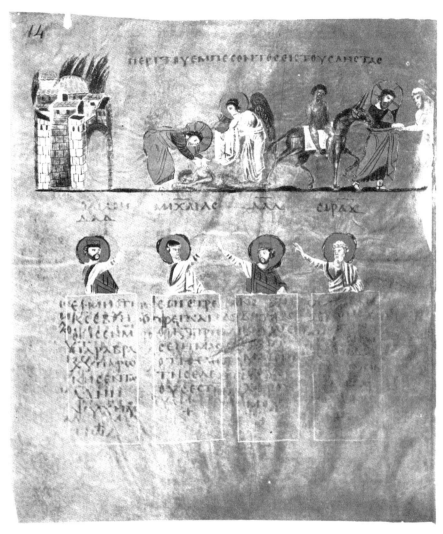

FIG. 25. Rossano, Cathedral Library, Rossano Gospels, Good Samaritan.

In the liturgical use of the illustrated roll we meet a clear instance of the artist's and scribe's awareness of the difference between the reader's and the observer's points of view. There was read and displayed in the church service in southern Italy, from the tenth to the thirteenth century, a type of book, now called an Exultet roll, that contained, beside the text and music for a particular rite, some pictures illustrating the content of the liturgy. An example in the Vatican shows the priest at the pulpit reading from the roll (FIG. 26); a second image is of beekeepers at work (FIG. 27). The bees produce wax from which were made the candles used in the church ceremony; bees and wax are accordingly themes of the liturgical verses. As the priest unrolls the text in reading, he exposes these pictures to the faithful. For the priest these are upside down, but they are directly legible to the lay viewers before him who cannot read the text. The written word and the musical notation that accompanies it are seen by them inverted. Together these two parts of the roll reflect a distinction between reader and viewer within the picture field that determines the opposed orientations of the written word and the picture.

More often the represented roll, apart from the inscription and even without it, seen as the vehicle of a speech-text, becomes, as mentioned earlier, a sign and bearer of dramatic relations in a narrative image. In the painting of Christ's Temptation by the Devil in the Goslar manuscript (FIG. 28), in the great letter L at the beginning of Matthew's Gospel, *Liber Generationis*, both Christ and the Devil carry rolls. The positions of the rolls change in the successive scenes, as if to match or symbolize a psychological development; but perhaps that variation is a purely artistic device

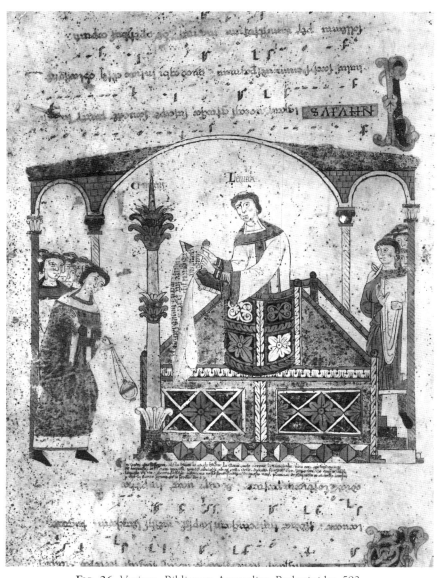

Fig. 26. Vatican, Biblioteca Apostolica, Barberini lat. 592,
Exultet Roll, Censing of Candle.

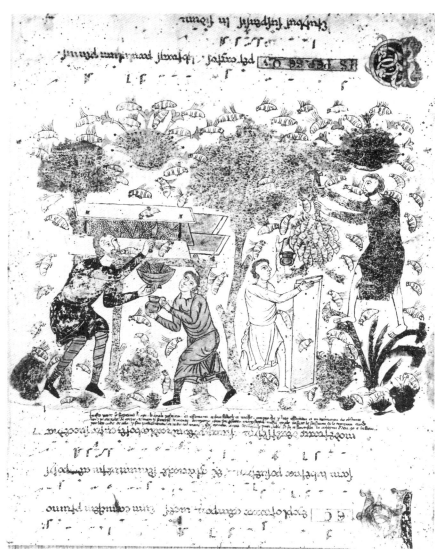

FIG. 27. Vatican, Barberini Lat. 592, Exultet Roll, Beekeeping Scene.

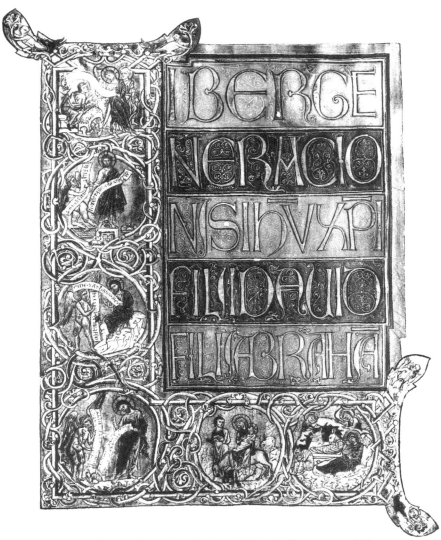

FIG. 28. Goslar, Rathaus, Gospels, Initial "L" with Temptation of Christ.

to express an ongoing dialogue of opposed wills without defining a more particular content. Each roll is of immense length, and the two cross, approach one another, and diverge; they are inscribed with the speeches of Jesus and the Devil. We can hardly imagine a pantomime produced today in which actors would carry rolls in that manner. In medieval art the theatrical concept of the "role" of each figure is made evident, concrete through his bearing a roll with writing that need not appear to be legible to either of the two actors. Their words turn in opposite directions. The speeches of both move from left to right; but the reading of the left-to-right order would entail a shifting of viewpoint for the figure to whom the speech is addressed, if we interpreted the relation of script to the inner viewer according to a realistic perspective. It is the sign for *speech* recognized as such rather than the internal viewer's reading of the written word that matters. *Word* and figure are juxtaposed here as the *en face* eye beside the profiled nose in archaic representations.

A more radical example in the same manuscript is the picture of the meeting of Mary and Elizabeth after the Annunciation (FIG. 29). Together they carry a single roll that is divided lengthwise by a line through the middle; Mary's speech moves downward on the left side and Elizabeth's upward on the right. Both maintain the invariant direction of Western script in accord with the position of each figure as a reader. While addressing each other, either woman can receive her cousin's words; but the distinction of two voices in a dialogue and their partnership as reciprocal speakers and hearers are made visible and reinforced through that paradoxical partitioning of the joint roll.

Where one person communicates to another, the artist will

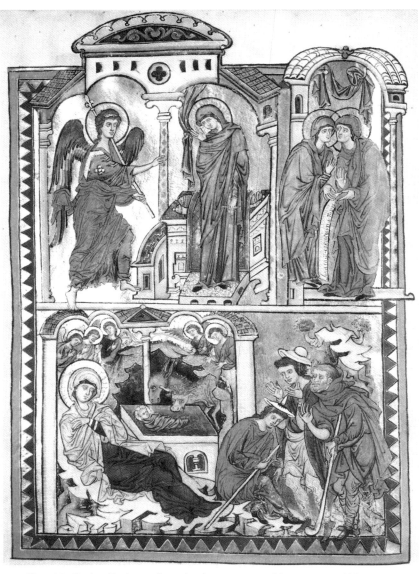

Fig. 29. Goslar, Rathaus, Gospels, Annunciation, Visitation, and Nativity.

sometimes represent a single roll extending from the hand of the first to the hand of the second. In a miniature painting, in the Cleveland Museum, from a Mosan center, Saint Gregory dictates his commentary on the Book of Job to the scribe at the right, who, with open book, receives the word and prepares to write (FIG. 30). The voiced communication is materialized here as a tangible connecting instrument in space. Observe that the roll is bent and pleated; through that fold is produced a recession in depth—the scribe is farther from us. Sitting on a pedestal, his head rises above the level of the saint's, as if seen from a higher viewpoint. Above, in a scene of Job and his friends, their conversation is implied in the bare rolls.

Where three persons are engaged in talk, as in a manuscript in the British Library, a single roll may circulate among them and unite them: a king, a bishop, and an abbot (FIG. 31). Below, a kneeling monk carries a wavy scroll behind his back in a dance-like, acrobatic manner; he seems to see and hear what is going on above; the scroll is perhaps identified with the scribe who records their talk.

Without writing, the roll may symbolize by its form alone the specific content of a thought. In a painting of the Supper at Emmaus in an English manuscript written toward 1200, Jesus, after revealing himself to the seated pilgrims, ascends through a cloud (FIG. 32). They now recognize Jesus, whom they had not known at first, although they were his disciples. The two rolls they hold to signify their speech cross and form an **X**—not in conflict, however, but to signify, I suppose, a meeting or coincidence of minds in their recognition of Christ. Another example of writing that conveys thought is found in an early miniature in

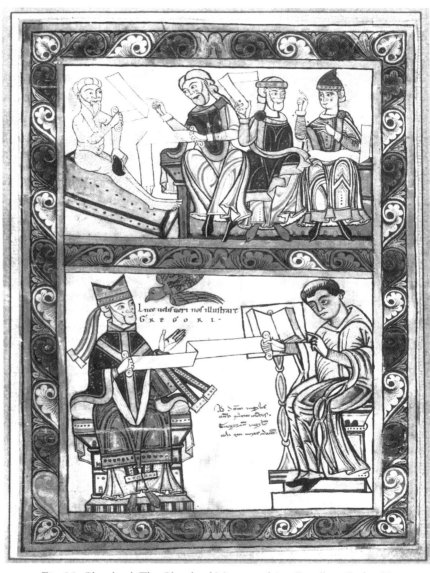

Fig. 30. Cleveland, The Cleveland Museum of Art, Engelbert Codex 20,
Title page of "Moralia of Gregorius."

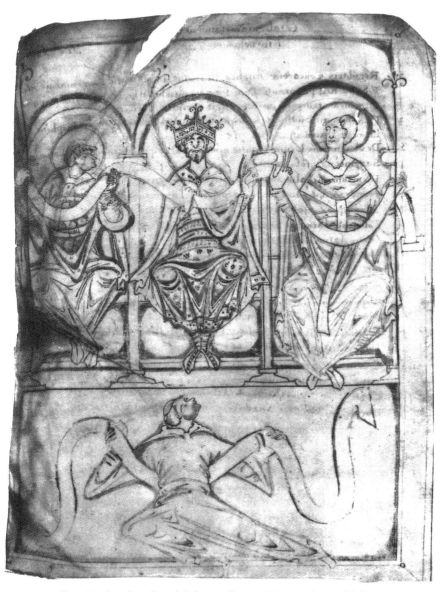

FIG. 31. London, British Library, Cotton Tiberius A. iii., fol. 2v.

167

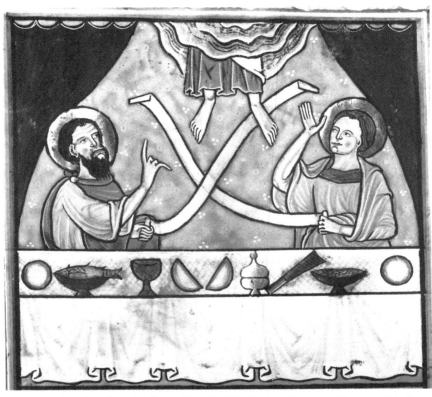

FIG. 32. London, British Library, Royal I.D.X., Psalter, Supper at Emmaus, fol. 5b.

the Stuttgart Psalter, which shows a figure plowing (FIG. 33). We read, inscribed above his head, his call to the animal: *ara, ara*—"plow, plow!" Although the writing is outside the border, beyond the edge of the background, it does not mean it was added later, as has been suggested. On other pages of the same book you will see elements of the picture that cross the frame. The plowman's hand rises above the edge of the landscape as does his robe.

That speech, though not a visible object, can be brought to the eye is intimated in a drawing in the richly illustrated Albani Psalter (FIG. 34). The initial of the Forty-fourth Psalm shows David with pen in hand, pointing to his tongue; the accompanying text reads: "My tongue is the pen of a swift scribe." The tongue, the instrument of speech, is identified here with the pen. When you speak, you write, as it were, in the air. The authorizing metaphor creates a problem for the artist; how to distinguish the speech act, the invisible writing produced by the tongue, from the writing that the artist appends or inserts as a label for the picture or as a passage from the Gospel transmitting an already recorded speech.

A characteristic solution is in an English manuscript of the thirteenth century, the Life of St. Alban: in the scene of the digging up of the saint's bones, a witness, happy at the discovery, chants *Te Deum laudamus*—"We praise thee, God" (FIG. 35). The words issue from near his mouth and move upward around his head. Next to him is a bishop beside whose nose we read the strange word *redolet*—"it is fragrant." It is the odor of sanctity that he smells when the true bones of the martyr are uncovered. Here not only is speech made visible but also the curved vector of speech and something of its sense. The relation of the words to

Posuit flumina in desertum & exitus aquarum sitim

terra fructifera infalsuginem amaricia habitancium in ea

Posuit desertum in stagna aquarum

& terra sine aqua in exitus aquarum

Et collocauit illic esurientes

& constituerunt ciuitatem habitationis

Et seminauerunt agros & plantauer uineas

& fecerunt fructum natiuitatis

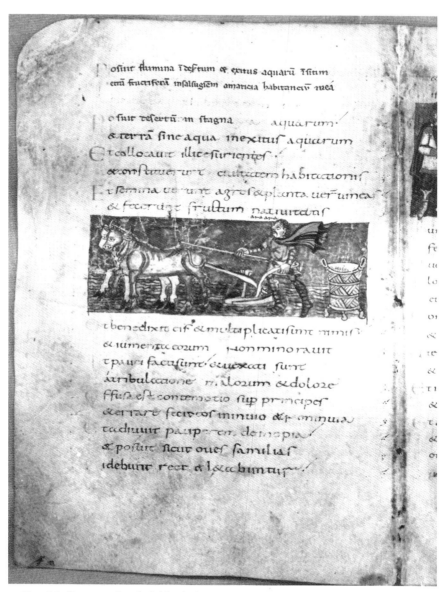

& benedixit eis & multiplicati sunt nimis

& iumenta eorum non minorauit

& pauci facti sunt & uexati sunt

a tribulatione malorum & dolore

Effusa est contemptio super principes

& errare fecit eos in inuio & non in uia

& adiuuit pauperem de inopia

& posuit sicut oues familias

& uidebunt recti & laetabuntur

FIG. 33. Stuttgart, Landesbibliothek, Stuttgart Psalter, MS 23, Plowing, fol. 124v.

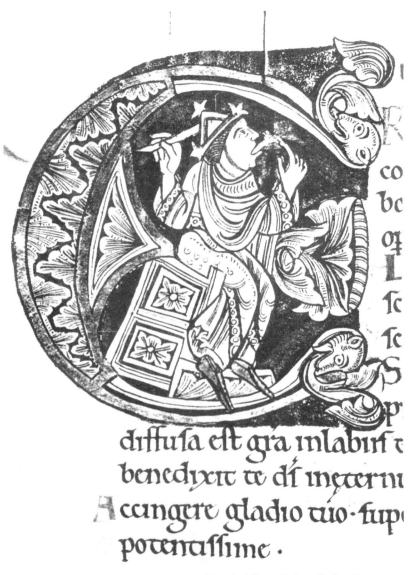

diffufa eft gra inlabirf t
benedixit te dí ineterni
Accingere gladio tuo · fup(
potentiffime ·

FIG. 34. Hildesheim, Bibl. S. Godehard, Albani Psalter, Psalm 44,
"The Tongue is the pen of a swift stroke."

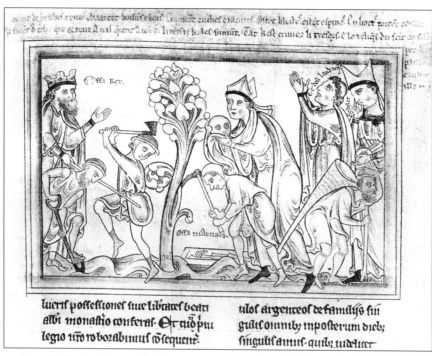

FIG. 35. Dublin, Trinity College, Life of St. Alban, MS E.1.40, Finding the body.

what they designate has been mimicked in their forms—a remarkable, naive effort to represent graphically a directed process of sound and smell. The script is oriented with reference to the source, goal, and meaning of a speech act, unlike the static horizontal transcriptions of the names of figures in the same field. One can collect other examples and through them reconstitute medieval beliefs about the senses and language.

Not only was human speech represented visually but also the "speech" of animals, their cries and calls: they were even shown learning to read like the modern monkeys who are trained to distinguish written signs and respond to them. In an English miniature a bear tamer tries to teach the alphabet to his beast (FIG. 36). From the man's mouth issue the letters, A, B, C; from the bear's comes only an A. One remembers the eleventh-century story of the cleric who wished to teach a wolf to pronounce those letters; he tells him to say A, and the wolf says "Agnus"; that's all he can think of—he connects the initial with the prey nearest to his desire.

That visual rendering of speech in the Middle Ages may be matched on Greek vases. On an often cited one, made shortly before 500 B.C., are painted three young men who see a swallow; one cries: "How lovely!"; another: "Spring is here" (FIG. 37). A swallow flies above them; their speech, issuing from very near the mouth, is directed upward to the air. In a related stage of that earlier culture, with a comparable growth of pictorial fancy, speech was depicted as a visible element of a pictured episode, no less concrete for the viewer than the speakers and the objects of their talk.

A medieval example of spoken argument in a formal debate is a

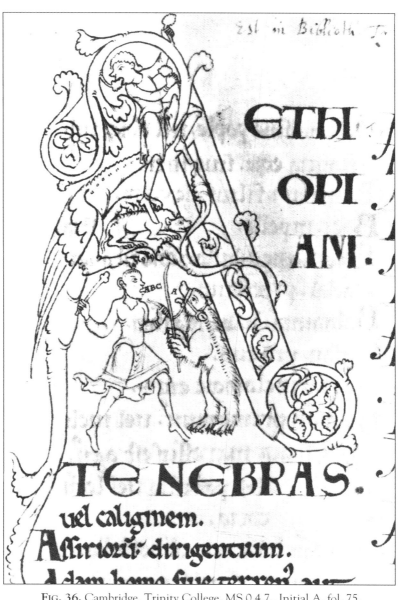

FIG. 36. Cambridge, Trinity College, MS 0.4.7., Initial A, fol. 75.

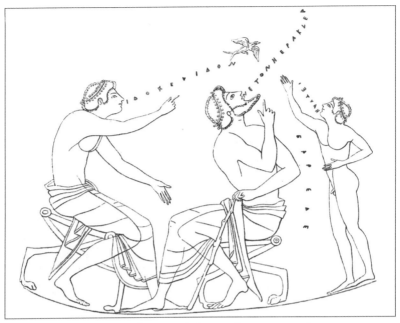

FIG. 37. Greek vase with figures observing a swallow.

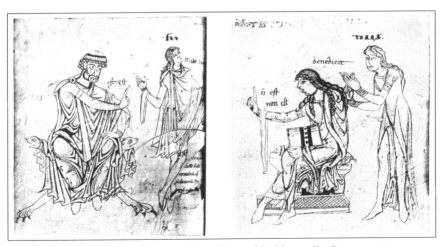

FIG. 38. Austria, Klosterneuberg, Hugo of St. Victor, De Sacramentis,
MS 311, f. 82v and 83.

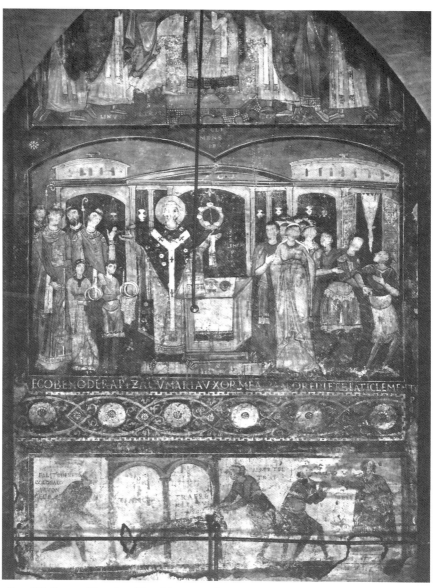

FIG. 39. Rome, Church of San Clemente, fresco, Speeches of Sisinnius and workmen.

drawing from Klosterneuburg (Austria) in a manuscript of Hugo of St. Victor on the sacraments (FIG. 38). The seated princely figure at the left says, *est, est* ("it's so, it's so"); the other, a woman with legs crossed, says *n[on] est, non est* and makes a gesture of dispute. But unlike John and Arius in the Anglo-Saxon drawing, the subject of their dispute is not conveyed; it is an image of assertion and negation as a polarized pair of which the opposition is also expressed in the **X**-symmetry of postures and attributes and even in the pairing of male and female partners. At their sides stand supporting figures, a woman with crossed legs at the left, a man at the right. The inscription is cut in half; over one we read, FAU, over the other, TORES; together they spell *fautores*—the applauders, the two claques.

For the popular element in pictures with inscribed speech, there is an example that belongs to the history of the Italian language as well as art. It is one of the oldest documents of Italian vernacular speech. In a scene in a fresco of the underground Church of San Clemente in Rome the pagan prefect, Sisinnius, whose wife had been converted to Christianity by Clement, pursues her in Clement's church and is struck blind and deaf (FIG. 39). He appears again below, commanding his servants to bind and carry off the saint. Pretending to obey him, they tie a column that they prepare to carry off, lifting it with a crowbar. The inscription of his orders to them reads: "Pull, you sons of whores" (*fili de le pute*). Another inscription, set behind the crowbar, quotes a worker: "Turn it as you lift" (*falite dereto colo palo, carvoncelle*). Here, in words that are Italian already, though still close to Latin, we meet vernacular speech: an inscription on and below the arches is in a different and somewhat better Latin.

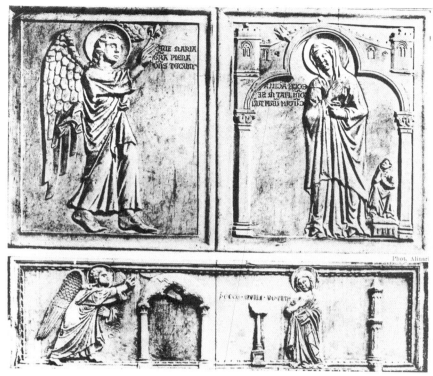

FIG. 40. San Miniato al Tedesco, Cathedral, Giroldo da Como, relief, Annunciation.

The representation of words issuing from the mouth of a speaker entailed an interesting anomaly of script. If the profile head faced the left, how would the artist render the fact of emission of the voice?

In a Tuscan relief sculpture of the thirteenth century in the Church of San Miniato al Tedesco by an artist who signed his name, Giraldo, on the work, the Virgin answers the angel's *"Ave gratia plena"* with *"Ecce Ancilla domini"* inscribed from right to left (Fig. 40). Is it inscribed backward simply to conform to the direction of her speech as emitted, or has the reversal another significance? Since early times, the church fathers (and later interpreters) had observed that in the angel's speech to Mary his first word, *Ave*, is the reverse of *Eva*. Eve's sin doomed the human race, and the Virgin, by accepting the Incarnation, helped to redeem it. That idea of the mirror symmetry of Eve–Ave in the coupling and contrast of Eve and Mary and their final unit in the redemption of mankind could have suggested the reversal in the inscription. Just as Eve's guilt is reversed by Mary, so in their written form Mary's words of acceptance are reversed in direction. I don't know how to explain this phenomenon of reversal otherwise, though in certain contexts reversal has a demonic sense. In a scene of Peter's martyrdom on a capital in Moissac the name of Nero is written backward, to indicate his evil nature. Incantations are sometimes recited backward; so, too, are numbers in magic: 1, 2, 3, 3, 2, 1. Reversal there may have a magic countermagical function. It inhabits the breaking of the spell by the opponent: you have done it first and you are protected. But in the inscription of Giraldo, reversal has its own special meaning, which one understands in the light of that long tradition of Eva–Maria.

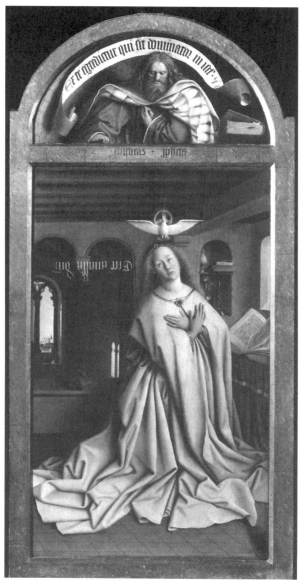

Fig. 41. Brussels, Cathedral, Jan van Eyck, Ghent Altarpiece, Annunciation.

A more familiar instance are Mary's words in Jan van Eyck's *Annunciation* on the Ghent altarpiece. Her reply, *"ecce ancilla domini,"* issuing from her mouth, is written backward and also inverted, as if addressed to God above or to the Holy Spirit (Fig. 41). In contrast to that inversion, the angel's speech from left to right is erect and overlaps some objects. It is a striking example of the recognized relativity of directions in space, depending on the position of an internal viewer.

What I have presented so far is characteristically medieval. It marks an art in which the bond with language determines some pictorial features; painting, then, is like language in its sequential narrative order, its literalness, and its submission to symbolism. Founded on texts, the image admits the written word as a concrete component free to rotate in the two dimensions of the picture plane.

The later Renaissance ideal of painting—as an image coherent to the eye with a unifying perspective—did not exclude the written word altogether from pictures. It was still admitted in emblems and certain religious themes of state. It reappeared at times even in purely secular subjects, especially where strong emotion impelled the artist to speak of himself in the painting. Two examples by Francisco Goya, an artist steeped in the powerful tradition of naturalistic pantomime and in physiognomic scenes of action, show how one could break through the constraints of the eusynoptic ideal within the framework of a most refined and searching painterly style.

In the gripping picture of himself attended by his doctor during

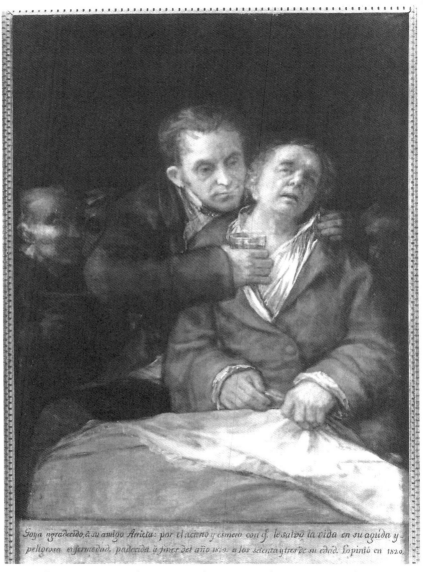

Goya agradecido, á su amigo Arrieta: por el acierto y esmero con q.ᵉ le salvó la vida en su aguda y peligrosa enfermedad, padecida á fines del año 1819. á los setentaytres de su edad. Lo pintó en 1820.

FIG. 42. Minneapolis, Minneapolis Institute of Arts, Francisco Goya, *Self-Portrait with Dr. Arrieta*, 1820.

182

a near-fatal sickness—a portrait situation unique in art—he has inscribed below the image, on the full breadth of the canvas, his "gratitude to his friend and doctor, Arrieta, for the sureness and care with which he saved Goya's life from the acute and dangerous illness suffered at the age of 73" (FIG. 42). The words are painted below on a tawny yellowish ground matched to the pallor of Goya's skin and in subtle accord with the red and green tones of the portrait. Yet the inscription does not belong to the space of the realistically pictured scene or to the frame. To read it we must shift our attention to what is visually of another order than the absorbing image above. Because of the poignant occasion, Goya was willing to inject a distracting and artistically incongruous element addressed to the viewer in order to explain and record forever that deeply disturbing climactic experience.

In an earlier painting, a portrait of the duchess of Alba, Goya had traced on the ground at her feet the two inverted words: *solo Goya* (FIGS. 43a and 43b). They refer not only to the painter but to his love of the portrayed person. What do they mean? Goya alone, only Goya? They seem also to say: I, Goya, your servant, your lover, am at your feet, on the ground. They are more than a signature addressed to the external viewer as a reader. The woman he portrays points to the words, which are impressed in the soil upside down for *her* to read and are fitted at the same time to the perspective reality of the external viewers' pictured space. The subject, as in the self-portrait, is also a matter of the heart, a moving personal revelation. The two words are an avowal addressed to the woman as both subject and ultimate viewer of the painting—a doubling and interlacing of the objective and the subjective, fascinating to the imagination. Through

183

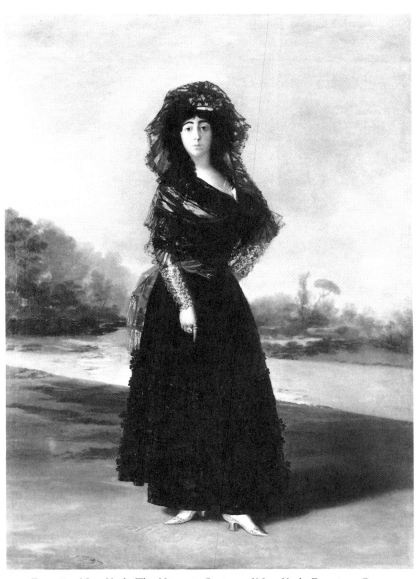

FIG. 43a. New York, The Hispanic Society of New York, Francisco Goya, *The Dutchess of Alba*, 1797.

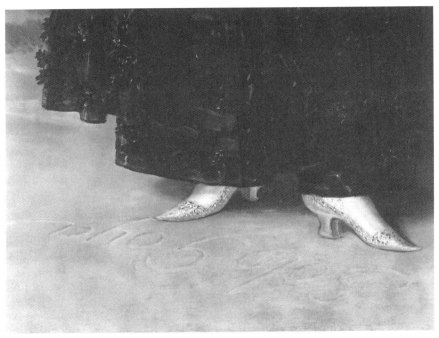

New York, The Hispanic Society of New York, Francisco Goya, *The Dutchess of Alba* (detail), 1797.

tate aute illa . multi crediderunt in eum samarita
norum . ppter uerbum mulieris testimoniu phiben
tis . quia dixit mihi omnia quecuq; feci Cum ue
nissent ergo adillum samaritani . rogauerunt eu
ut ibi maneret · Et mansit ibi duos dies · Et multi
plures crediderunt ppter sermone eius . et muli
eri dicebant · Quia iam non ppter tua loquelam
credimus . ipsi enim audiuimus et scimus . quia hic
est uere saluator mundi ·

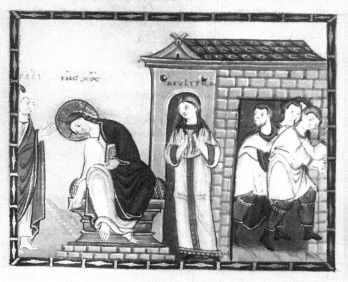

FIG. 44. Trier, Stadtbibliothek, MS 24, Codex Egberti,
Christ and the Adulterous Woman, fol. 46v.

the inscription, Goya speaks to her and commands her response. A later owner of the picture was embarrassed by the inscription and covered the telltale word *solo*; it has been disclosed only in recent years.

In these two works of Goya we see how devices of medieval painters, arising from their habitual engagement with the word, can be revived spontaneously in later art when a painter communicates through his art with an imaged object of his devotion, as in an ex-voto, or records with feeling his own salvation, the fortunate outcome of a frightening experience. Before these two paintings we may ask whether the requirement of a strictly unified, homogeneous visual language is inherent or necessary in art. Is it not an ideal arising in a certain style of objectivity, with a particular norm of truth to nature and visual perception in art of the sixteenth to the eighteenth century? Yet even that inscription in the portrait of the duchess of Alba may be viewed as a realistic trompe l'oeil effect, a consistent rendering of a material reality, a verbal message imprinted on the soft soil of the ground in a perspective coherent with the rest of the image. It belongs to the simulated reality of its pictured three-dimensional space rather than to the canvas surface, like an ordinary signature. At the same time, it signifies the active presence of the artist in that space as both a speaking self and an operating hand.

There is a German medieval picture with writing on the ground addressed to an internal reader as in Goya's portrait of the duchess of Alba. In the miniature painting of the adulterous woman in a Gospel lectionary of the tenth century, the Egbert Codex, the accusers bring her before Christ and call for his judgment (FIG. 44). He does not reply aloud but, inclining to the

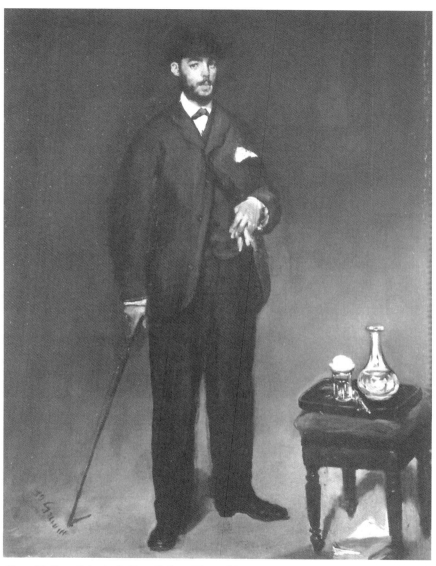

FIG. 45. Paris, Musée du Petit-Palais, Edouard Manet, *Portrait of Theodore Duret*, 1889.

ground, writes with his finger on the dust three words not recorded in the Gospel: *terra terram accusat*, "earth accuses earth" (or dirt accuses dirt = flesh accuses flesh). His pointing finger touches the last letter, as if to indicate his act of writing. In the Gospel account, he then rises and says, "Let him who has not sinned cast the first stone" (John 8:3–8). The diagonal inscription in the miniature is in perspective and hardly legible to the external viewer directly. It is not written horizontally across the field like other inscriptions in the miniatures of this manuscript. It is the only inscription of speech in the entire series of Gospel scenes. But these are not really spoken words; by calling upon the accusers to read his mute writing, Christ evokes in them a corresponding inner speech, the voice of conscience. One may also interpret the act of writing as a simulation of the written law— Christ in this episode lays down the law of forgiveness.

The significance and interest of Goya's signature in his portrait of the duchess was not lost to later artists. Indebted to Goya's example, I believe, was Manet in signing his portrait of Théodore Duret (FIG. 45). The subject points with his cane to the inscription at his feet, which is tilted upward and inverted, as if intended solely for his own eye. Manet could have seen Goya's picture when it was in the Spanish Museum of Louis-Philippe in the Louvre or later in private collections in Paris. Duret was the author of a book on Manet and one of his patrons and defenders. It has been suggested that the painter, by inverting the signature, was reminding Duret that he had not always been friendly to Manet's art and was converted only recently. I shall risk another explanation: Manet, who was aware of the meaning of *manet* in Latin, could be playing here on the equivalence of "*manet* =

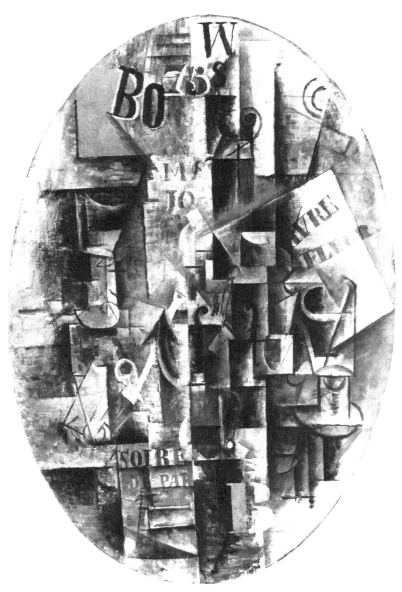

Fig. 46. Prague, Narodni Gallery, Picasso, *Violin, Glass, and Pipe on Table*, 1912.

durer"—a bilingual pun that implied the bond between the two men. The etcher Felix Bracquemond had inscribed a portrait of Manet in 1866: "manet et manebit"—he will endure.

In our own century the association of painting and script has enjoyed a new vogue through the example of the Cubists. These painters, whose works brought the most radical emancipation of their art from the bookish subject and from perspective, gave a prominent place on their canvases to bits of writing, to labels, newsprint, and musical scores. These signs were often segments of printed matter pasted on the picture surface. Here no conflict arises between modeled forms or the perspective of a scene in depth and the written or printed word attached on that surface. The still-life objects that became the main themes of Cubist representation during the few years after 1911, when the written or presented word was an element of the painting, are themselves decomposed into layered planes parallel to the surface or overlapping in a shallow depth. They are marked by discontinuous and intersecting lines, straight and curved, like the alphabetic forms of the musical notation. These, too, are generally fragments; often only part of a word is presented, but enough to incite the viewer to complete the whole, as in *Jour*[nal] (FIG. 46). They are artificial signs, instruments of communication, as the still-life objects are instruments of music and conviviality. At the same time, while seeking an austerely constructed order and engaging the viewer in contemplation of multiplied and ever-shifting relations of strokes and marks, lines and tones, often ambiguous or paradoxical when

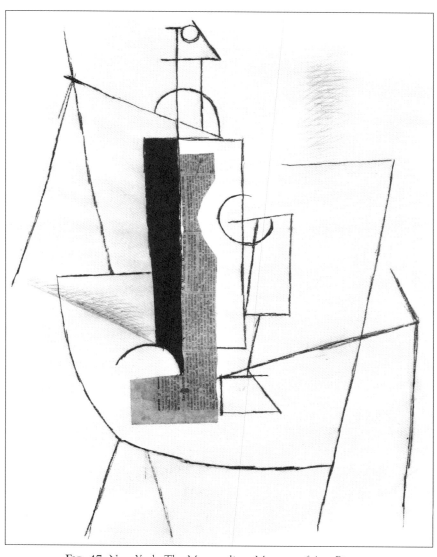

FIG. 47. New York, The Metropolitan Museum of Art, Picasso,
Still Life: Bottle and Glass on Table, 1912-13.

viewed as elements of a representation, the artists—Pablo Picasso and Georges Braque—turn a segment of newsprint 90° or more from its normal axis; we cannot read the text without twisting our necks or rotating the picture (FIG. 47). The words are not directed to an internal reader as in the anomalous medieval paintings. They form a surface pattern of the black units in regular alignment that we recognize as a word without our having to scan its parts or elements. In paradoxical contrast to both the medieval and the Cubist painting, the newsprint on paper is a bit of concrete material pasted to the surface in real relief, unlike the painted surface that, though not a perspective view, evokes by its simulation of overlapping planes, a shallow layered pictorial space, intricate, broken, and incompatible with the structure of the familiar space of tangible near objects. The layers form no well-ordered set of successive positions in an apparent three-dimensional space, with clear, determinable positions of each layer as a nearer or a farther, a before or behind, in a series.

We have seen earlier in a Renaissance printed book a trompe l'oeil page hanging from a high balcony on which stand the philosophers who stroll or converse (FIG. 1). Both elements—the figures and the suspended reading—appear wonderfully real in their large and small forms; but the printed page is the more tangible, the more substantial. In the Cubist painting the material reality of the written and printed words is allied to the no less marked concreteness of the strokes and touches that make up the painting, its lines, and its surface planes. It is not the represented objects but the material signs of the painter's ordered operations on the field of the canvas that claim our attention and make for the interest of the whole. Script, printed matter, marks, strokes,

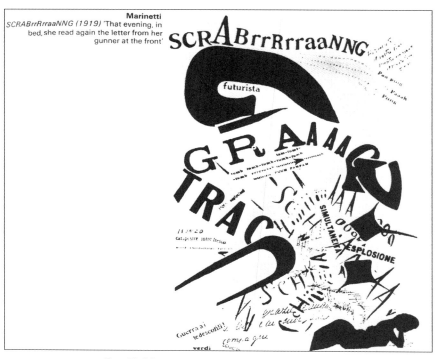

Fig. 48. Marinetti, SCRABrrRrraaNNG, 1919.

lines, flecks, are visible alike, and if they have a common matrix in the glasses, bottles, pipes, books, playing cards, musical instruments, and newspapers that are discernible in the work—all these may be taken as metaphors of the artistic intention and outlook. They are things from the quotidian reality, objects of manipulation without a fixed place or position, though static; they owe their existence and position to momentary and randomly placed, yet habitual, choices and manipulation by the individual, and they serve his senses. Beyond this special role of the still-life objects, there is finally the structure of the letter, the written word as an artifact in a style of the time, a rule-bound succession of a few elementary shapes—straight lines and simple curves, along a fixed axis—from which one can generate an infinity of different statements—grammatical, meaningful, communicative, as the Cubist painter constructs with a few simple types of form his artistically ordered and varied pictures.

In Cubist paintings, the break with the regular horizontal and vertical order of script is not a return to the medieval practice in which the aligned words follow the axes of a margin or frame. In the modern works the letters are often strewn at liberty without an apparent ruling principle other than an improvised effect of movement, scatter, liberty, and caprice. While the Cubists justify the deviation from the strict vertical and horizontal by the resulting coherence with the irregular segment of newsprint (or other object) to which the letters are attached, the words retaining their constraint by the orthogonals of a matrix as the whole is rotated, other artists of the time take pleasure in isolating and scrambling the elements of a word, a phrase, or a sentence from each other, and varying the axis of each (and often its size)—a

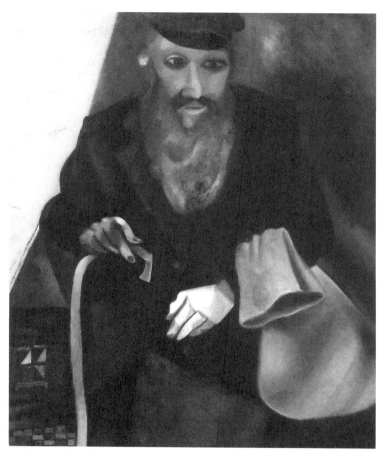

FIG. 49. Basel, Karl and Jürg Im Obersteg Collection, Marc Chagall,
The Jew in Red, 1919.

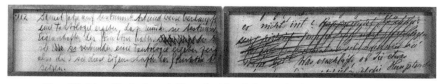

FIG. 50. New York, Joseph Kosuth, *Untitled Mistake (Discussed)* #2, 1990.

196

practice favored especially by the Futurists in their taste for an explosive form (FIG. 48).

The Futurists' practice is allusive in both the form and meaning of the scattered words, which are often designed to shake up the reader. Together these words celebrate with explosive energy the freedom, spontaneous movement, and noisy clamor of the contemporary metropolis, as features of an advancing modernity.

The general principle of the "words at liberty," proclaimed by the Futurist Filippo Tommaso Marinetti as a visual equivalent to the freedom of verse in both form and sense, could be applied in a painting for other ends, even to affirm a feeling for tradition and community.

Something of the sacredness of the word in medieval art returns in a painting of 1914 (*The Jew in Red*) by Marc Chagall in the Karl and Jürg Im Obersteg Collection (FIG. 49). He has inscribed on the background a floating set of words, the names of his most venerated painters. The words are tilted at different angles and written in three alphabets: "Giotto" and "Peasant Brueghel (Brueghel Muzhik)" are in Russian characters; the name of Rembrandt, so dear to Jewish sensibility, is in Hebrew letters reading from right to left; in Latin script are "Cezanne," "Tintoretto," "Courbet," "Fouquet," and others. They are Chagall's personal gallery of great "Latin" masters among whom he marks certain ones as his affinities, his deepest loves, the saints or prophets of his art, by writing their names in their own alphabets. In isolating that litany of artists' names, Chagall departs from the Cubist practice of Picasso and Braque, for whom the reading matter in a painting belongs to the same intimate sphere of the vernacular, everyday, artificial, and quotidian as the still-

197

life objects among which they are embedded and to which they are related by their recurrent elementary forms. Those inscribed names of great artists are a more direct personal allusion; they bespeak the self-consciousness of the painter who, through those scattered names, affirms both his venerated heritage of past art and his own family line as a cosmopolitan Russian Jew, like the subject of the picture. In another portrait he transcribes a lengthy passage from Genesis in Hebrew letters that fill a considerable part of the canvas.

In more recent decades, script has spread over the entire surface as a message of what is called conceptual art. Penned ideas about art have replaced the preceding painted colors and drawn or constructed forms (FIG. 50). The polarity of the written sign and the image construction has been resolved by the restriction to a written discourse as an object of art in itself.

PHOTO CREDITS